Rays from the Sun of Righteousness

RAYS

FROM THE

SUN OF RIGHTEOUSNESS

SERMONS FOR CHILDREN

ON

THE UNSEARCHABLE RICHES OF CHRIST

RICHARD NEWTON

Author of *Heroes of the Early Church,*
Heroes of the Reformation, The King's Highway etc.

SOLID GROUND CHRISTIAN BOOKS
BIRMINGHAM, ALABAMA USA

Solid Ground Christian Books
2090 Columbiana Rd, Suite 2000
Birmingham, AL 35216
205-443-0311
sgcb@charter.net
http://solid-ground-books.com

RAYS FROM THE SUN OF RIGHTEOUSNESS
Sermons for Children on the Unsearchable Riches of Christ

Richard Newton (1813-1887)

Taken from 1876 edition by T. Woolmer, London, England

Solid Ground Classic Reprints

First printing of new edition March 2006

Cover work by Borgo Design, Tuscaloosa, AL
Contact them at nelbrown@comcast.net

*Special thanks to Ric Ergenbright for permission to use
the image on the cover. Visit him at ricergenbright.org*

ISBN: 1-59925-062-4

PREFACE.

It is now about twenty-five years since the writer of this little book published his first volume of sermons for the young. That volume was called 'Rills from the Fountain of Life.' It was intended to help young persons who were trying to serve God and find their way to heaven. He has since been permitted to publish a number of similar volumes. These have all had the same object in view. This present volume differs from the others in one thing; viz., that the sermons in it are all especially occupied in telling about the Lord Jesus Christ. They speak of Him as the Sun of Righteousness, as the Light of the World, as the Bright and Morning Star; and so on all through the volume.

It is the hope of the writer that this may prove the best and most useful of all his books. He cherishes this hope for the reason that the book is all about the blessed Saviour. The knowledge of Him is the most important of all knowledge. There are so many things for us to know about Jesus; and these are all so full of meaning, and the meaning is so very important, that we may go on studying them as long as we live, and we shall always find in them something fresh and interesting and profitable. Saint Paul tells us that the *love* of Christ 'passeth knowledge.' He means by this that we never can take it all in, never get to the end or the bottom of it. In studying it, we are like persons sailing over an ocean that has no shore. We might go sailing on for ever. And what Saint Paul said of the *love* of Christ is just as true of His power, and wisdom, and grace, and goodness. They are all 'past finding out.' We cannot find them out fully, though we may in part.

And if this is so, then nothing can be more useful to us than that which helps us to find out the treasures of love and grace and knowledge that are hidden in Jesus.

If God shall bless this volume by making it the means of leading some who read it, whether young or old, to think more of Jesus, and try to love and serve Him better, the writer will feel amply rewarded.

R. N.

May, 1876.

CONTENTS.

'BLESSED BE THE GREAT AUTHOR OF LIGHT! TO-DAY I HAVE ONCE
MORE LOOKED UPON THE SUN.'—*See page* 24.

I.

JESUS THE SUN OF RIGHTEOUSNESS.

' The Sun of Righteousness shall rise with healing in His wings.',
MALACHI iv. 2.

WE begin now a new course of sermons for the young. This will be about the character and work of Jesus. We shall take up some of the different names and titles by which He is made known to us in the Bible. And if we consider Jesus as the Sun that gives us all our light and life, and warmth and blessing, then every passage of Scripture that tells us anything about Him may be regarded as a beam of light from this Sun. And so we may call these sermons *Rays from the Sun of Righteousness.* And before going on to speak of these rays, it will be proper to speak about Jesus as the Sun from whom they shine forth. For this purpose we have taken these words from the prophet Malachi as our text for the first sermon in this course :—

'The Sun of Righteousness shall rise with healing in His wings.'

'The Sun of Righteousness' here spoken of means Jesus. This is one of the names or titles given to Him, or one of the figures made use of in the Bible, to show us what Jesus is to His people, or what He does for them. And the question for us to consider now is, What is it that the sun does, on account of which

Jesus may well be compared to it? There are three things that the sun does, or three kinds of power that the sun exercises, which show us how well Jesus may be compared to the sun.

The FIRST *power that the sun exercises is a* GREAT DRAWING POWER. And for this reason Jesus is like the sun.

Men call this great power the *attraction* of the sun. Now, to attract means to draw. The attracting power of the sun is the power which it has of drawing things to it.

The sun has a number of large worlds around it. It stands in the centre of these worlds, like a father in the midst of his family. These worlds all move round the sun, and are kept in their places by the drawing power which the sun exerts. And all the worlds, in the family of worlds to which our globe belongs, feel this power of the sun. The least of them feels it, and the largest of them feels it. The one that is nearest to him feels it, and the one that is farthest off from him feels it too. The world in our family that is the farthest off from the sun is the planet Neptune. We cannot see him with our naked eye. This far-off brother of ours is about twenty-eight hundred millions of miles away from us. We can form no idea how many there are in *one* million; much less can we form any idea of these hundreds of millions. But just let us make one calculation, to find out how long it would take us to go from our earth to the planet Neptune. Suppose there was a railway from our earth reaching away off to that distant world, and suppose we could get into a car here, and set off to visit our outside brother Neptune. Suppose the train was a through train, and was to travel at the rate of thirty miles an hour, night and day, without stopping : how long do you think it would take to get there ? Perhaps some of you may think it would be a nice trip to take some summer vacation. A summer vacation, indeed ! Why, it would take us more than a *thousand years* to get there, travelling all the time at thirty miles an hour. Suppose we had started on this trip in the year in which our Saviour was born. Suppose we had only spent a few days on the planet Neptune, and then had started on our way back ; and suppose we had kept on travelling, night and day, at the same rate without stopping, ever since then, *we should not be back yet.* We should still have to travel on for *more than two hundred years* longer before we reached home.

And yet the sun has power to draw that far-off planet towards it, so that it never gets out of its place.

And Jesus is just like the sun in this respect. He has a wonderful power to draw people to Him. When He was on earth He said : ' And I, if I be lifted up, will *draw all men* unto Me.' (John xii. 32.) One thing meant by this *lifting up* of Jesus was His crucifixion. This was what He meant when He said : ' As Moses *lifted up* the serpent in the wilderness, even so must the Son of man be lifted up.' (John iii. 14.) When Jesus was crucified, He was nailed to the cross, and then lifted up on it, and left to hang there till He died. That was one way in which He was lifted up.

Another way in which He is lifted up is by telling people about Him. When a minister is preaching to His people about Jesus, or when a Sunday-school teacher is talking to his class about the love of Jesus in dying for us, then it may be said that both these persons are lifting up Jesus before those who hear them. And when Jesus says He would draw *all* men unto Him if He were lifted up, what He means is, *not* that every individual who hears about Him will be drawn to Him and be saved, but that men of *all kinds* will be made to feel the drawing power which He exercises, and so will be saved by Him.

If there were time to do so, it would be very easy to give illustrations to show how people of every kind have been drawn to Jesus by hearing the Gospel preached and taught. Rich people and poor people, young people and old people, learned people and ignorant people, have been thus drawn to Him.

Here is a story about something that took place at a mission school in South Africa. It shows how even young children may be drawn to Jesus themselves, and then may be made use of to draw others to Him. A man in Africa, who cared nothing for religion, was persuaded to send two of his children to the mission school: one of these was a boy eight years old, the other a girl of six. As the station was some distance from their home, the children had to board at the house of the missionary. After they had been there some time, however, the father wanted the boy to help him in taking care of the cattle; so he went to the school to take him away. But the little fellow had learned to love his teachers. He had become very fond of the lessons he was learning; and, above all, he was feeling his heart drawn to Jesus, and was beginning to love Him. He did not wish to go home, and told his father so, and begged that he might be allowed to stay. When asked the reason why he wished to stay, he said, ' Because I can't learn anything good at home.'

' And what good can such a child as you learn here ? ' asked his father.

' Father,' said the boy, ' I *have* learned something good here already.'

' What have you learned ? ' was the next question.

'I have learned this beautiful text: "This is a faithful saying, and worthy of all acceptation, that Christ Jesus came into the world to save sinners." And, father, I have learned who Jesus Christ is. He is the Son of God. Yes, father; and I have learned who sinners are. We are all sinners.'

These words of his little boy had such an effect on the father, that he went home alone and left his boy at the school; and in a few weeks he came back to the school a changed man. That one verse had drawn his heart to Jesus. He became a Christian, and was baptized.

John Wesley, the honoured founder of the Methodist branch of the Church, was once attacked by a robber, who demanded his money. After handing it to him, as the man was going away, Mr. Wesley called him back, and said: 'My friend, let me say a word to you. The time may come when you will be very sorry for the kind of life you are now leading. Remember, then, this passage from the Bible: "The blood of Jesus Christ His Son cleanseth from all sin." ' He said no more, and they parted.

Many years after, as Mr. Wesley was one day leaving a church where he had been preaching, a person came up to him, and asked if he remembered being robbed once in a particular place. 'I do,' said Mr. Wesley. 'I was the man who robbed you, Sir,' said the stranger. 'I wish to thank you for the words you spoke to me on that occasion. That sweet verse of Scripture that you quoted there took such hold of my mind, that I could never rest till I turned from my wicked ways in deep repentance, and became a Christian.' Jesus was lifted up to this robber when Mr. Wesley spoke those simple words to him; and that one text from the Bible was made the means of drawing that robber to Jesus.

But what is it in Jesus that draws men so ? It is His wonderful love in dying for us. Let me try to show you how this is.

There was a good Christian family in England. Mr. and Mrs. Stone were the names of the father and mother, and they had four little children. Mr. Stone's brother had died, leaving a little orphan boy, named Jack, about nine years old. As he was the boy's uncle and his nearest relative, Mr. Stone thought he ought to take him into his family, and bring him up among his own children; but Jack was such a wild, bad boy that he was afraid of the evil effect he might have on the other children. But finally it was concluded that Jack was to come, and so he came.

He had never been taught to obey, and he was very lawless and rude. But he had worse faults than these. He loved to tease and worry his little cousins. He had an ugly disposition, and sometimes broke out into very violent fits of temper, when he would destroy anything he could lay his hands on. Punishment had no effect. Reasoning and coaxing had no effect. His one answer to everything said to him was, ' *I don't care.*'

His cousin Susie was a gentle, delicate little thing. She felt very sorry for Jack, because no one loved him ; and she was always trying in some sweet, loving way to make him better. But one day he got very angry with her, and in his rage threw her doll into the fire, tore her hair, and actually scratched her arm till the blood came.

As a punishment for this, he was locked up in the lumber room, which was called ' the jail,' because it had iron bars across the windows, having been once used as a nursery. He was put on prisoner's fare, bread and water, till he should promise to do better. But he was cross and sullen, and had nothing to say but, ' *I don't care.'* Nobody felt so sorry for Jack as Susie did.

'Mother,' she said at night, 'I can't go to sleep for thinking of poor Jack, all alone, with no light, and nothing;' and her little lip quivered.

The third day had come, and Jack showed no signs of sorrow for his fault. *'I don't care'* was all he would say. 'Mother,' said Susie, 'mayn't I go and be shut up, while Jack comes out to see how pleasant it is? There is no sun there, nor anything.'

Her mother looked tenderly in the dear child's face, and said, 'Go, Susie.'

Susie went to Jack's door, and unlocking it said, 'I asked mother if I might come and take your place, Jack, while you go out and see how pleasant it is; it is so dismal and lonely here.'

Jack looked up and stared at her. 'What a fool you are!' said he. Then he walked slowly out, while Mrs. Stone came and locked Susie in. 'Let Jack take my dinner downstairs, mother,' whispered Susie, 'and I'll take *his* dinner up here.'

At dinner-time Jack took his seat opposite Susie's vacant chair. 'You can carry up Susie her bread and water,' said Mrs. Stone, handing him the tray. He took it and walked away, looking very sober, if not softened. According to Susie's wish, he stayed downstairs all the afternoon till supper-time.

After dark, he asked, 'Must Susie stay there all night, if I don't?' 'Yes,' said Mrs. Stone. Tears started into Jack's eyes. He ran upstairs, and darting into the jail-chamber he said : 'Susie, you are the very best girl I ever knew. Susie, I'll never, never treat you so again. I'm sorry,—I am. I'll try to be a good boy,—I will. Susie, what makes you so good to *me?* and he threw his arms round her neck, and cried as if

B

his heart would break. Jack was drawn to Susie. And what was it that drew him? It was her love to him. She showed this love by her willingness to suffer for him.

And it is just so with Jesus. He put Himself in our place. He suffered for us. He died for us. And when we come to see how wonderful the love was which led Him to do this for us, then we begin to feel the drawing power of Jesus. As the apostle says, it is ' the love of Christ that *constrains*,' or *draws* the hearts of people to Him.

And so, in the first place, the sun has a great drawing power, and for *this* reason Jesus is like it.

But, in the SECOND *place, the sun has a* GREAT HEALING POWER, and in this, too, it represents Jesus. The prophet Malachi says He shall ' rise with *healing in His wings*,' or beams.

During the night, while the sun is absent, the dew falls, and the mists gather and settle down. These make it damp, cold, and unhealthy. Agues and chills and many forms of sickness come from these causes. But when the sun arises, with his bright, warm beams, he dries up the dampness and drives away the mists, and by thus removing what would be sure to cause sickness it may well be said that he ' rises with *healing in his wings*.'

In some countries on the coasts of the Mediterranean Sea, every morning, about sunrise, a fine, fresh breeze sets in from the sea and blows across the land. It has such a good effect in scattering the mists and clouds that gather during the night, in driving away disease, and in promoting the health of the people, that they call this morning breeze ' *the doctor*.' And this breeze which the sun sets in motion may well be considered as the wings of the sun. And so it is literally true in those places that 'the sun arises with healing in his wings.'

I was reading the other day some extracts from the report of a physician connected with a hospital. He had a young girl under his care, who was suffering from consumption. At first, she was in a room where the bright, gladdening beams of the sun never shone. It was a damp, gloomy, cheerless room. And in spite of all that the doctor could do for her, he found that she was getting worse every day. At last, he ordered her room to be changed. She was removed to a bright, cheerful room, on which the sun shone for several hours a day. The doctor ordered her to sit in the sunbeams, and take a sun bath. She did so, and at once began to grow better. Thus it was true, in the case of that young girl, that ' the sun arose upon her with *healing in his wings.*' And so I suppose I may safely say that *sunshine is good for consumption.* Sunshine is good for nearly all diseases. I do not mean to say that sunshine alone will cure disease. No; but it is a great help to the physician in his blessed work of curing the sick. Suppose we should have no sunshine, all over the world for six months. What a dreadful effect it would have on the health of people generally ! The doctors would have their hands full of patients, and would find it very hard to make them well. The medicines given would not cure people, as they had formerly done. They would seem to have lost their healing power. And the difficulty would be not in the medicines, but in the want of the sunshine. The sun is indeed a great doctor. It is just as true as can be that he rises every day ' with *healing in his wings.*'

And how beautifully the sun represents Jesus in this respect ! What healing power there is in Him !

Sin is a dreadful spiritual disease. It prevails every-where in our fallen world. And there is no power that can heal this disease, except what comes from Jesus, the Sun of Righteousness. The Bible is full of the beams of this blessed Sun. And when we read of some sweet text of Scripture leading a poor, sin-sick soul to Jesus, and of that soul finding healing and life in Him, then we see an illustration of what the prophet means when he speaks of 'the Sun of Righteousness rising with healing in His wings.' Let me give you one or two illustrations of the way in which this healing power of Jesus is often put forth.

One day a missionary in India was walking along, not very far from the river Ganges. The Hindus worship this river as a god. They think it the most blessed of all things to die on the banks of the Ganges, and within reach of its waters. When a person is sick, his friends, or the members of his family, will carry him to the brink of this river, and put an end to his illness and his life together, by stopping his mouth and nose with the mud of the river, and then leaving him on its bank, with his feet and limbs in the water of what they consider that sacred stream. The missionary of whom I am speaking, as he walked on, met a company of Hindus. They were carrying a sick man to the Ganges, to leave him there to die, or to put him to death in the way just spoken of. But the man was un-willing to go. He struggled hard against it, and kept saying: 'I don't want to go to the Ganges. I am not a heathen: I am a Christian. I won't have any Saviour but Jesus. The missionary interfered, and stopped the men from carrying out their purpose. He had the sick man carried to the mission station, where he was nursed and taken care of.

When the man got better, the missionary talked

with him, and asked him how he came to be a Christian.
He gave this account of himself :—

'One day,' said he, 'a number of years ago, I heard
a missionary preaching from the Bible. When he was
done, I went up to him, and asked him to give me a
copy of that book. He said he had none with him but
the one out of which he was preaching, and that he
could not part with it. I told him I must know something more about that book. Then he tore a blank leaf
out of the book, and wrote one verse in it. He handed
the leaf to me, and told me that if I made a right use
of it, that verse would lead me to heaven.' These were
the words of the verse : '*God so loved the world, that He
gave His only begotten Son, that whosoever believeth in Him
should not perish, but have everlasting life.*' 'This one
verse,' said the man, 'led me to Jesus, and made me a
Christian.' How interesting this is ! That one verse was
like a beam or ray from the Sun of Righteousness ; and
oh ! there was healing in that beam. It brought health
and salvation to the soul of that poor heathen.

Here is another illustration of the healing power that
goes forth from the beams of the Sun of Righteousness.

In a town in one of our western States, there was
a Roman Catholic family, consisting of the father and
mother and a little girl named Mary, about seven years
old. There was no Catholic church within reach, so
Mary was allowed to go to a Protestant Sunday-school.

The father of this family was taken suddenly very
sick. Thinking he was going to die, and knowing that
he was not ready, he became very much troubled about
his sins. One night he awoke, and was in such great
distress that he begged his wife to pray for him. She
said she had never prayed for herself, and did not know
how to pray.

'O, what shall I do for my poor soul ?' cried the sick

man. 'Perhaps,' said his wife, 'our little Mary can pray, for she has been going to the Sunday-school a good while.'

'Go and call her at once,' he said.

Her mother went upstairs to her room. Mary was fast asleep. She awoke her, wrapped a shawl round her, and carried her downstairs, and seated her on her father's bed.

'Mary, my child, can you pray?' asked her father, with great earnestness. 'O, yes, father, I can, she said. 'Will you kneel down and pray for your poor father?'

'Yes, I will pray for you.' So she kneeled down, and putting up her little hands she said: 'Our Father, which art in heaven,'—going through the Lord's prayer. Then she prayed in her own language. She asked God to have mercy on her father, to pardon his sins, and teach him to love Jesus, and to make him well again for Jesus' sake. When she had finished, her father said: 'Mary, will you read to me from the Bible?' 'Yes, I will, father,' she said. Then she got her Bible, and began to read the third chapter of St. John. She read on till she came to these words: 'As Moses lifted up the serpent in the wilderness, even so must the Son of man be lifted up, that whosoever believeth on Him should not perish, but have everlasting life.' When her father heard this, he said, 'O Mary, is *that* there?'

'Yes, father, it is here; and these are the very words that Jesus said.'

'Well, that is just what I want.'

'Yes, father; but hear the rest of it. "For God so loved the world, that He gave His only begotten Son, that whosoever believeth in Him should not perish, but have everlasting life."'

' O, that is for me, for a poor sinner like me. "Whosoever believeth in Him." I can believe in Him; I *do* believe in Him.' And from that night Mary's father became a happy and useful Christian. Those texts that Mary read from the Bible were like beams from the Sun of Righteousness, and they brought healing to the soul of that poor man. The sun has a great healing power. And Jesus is like the sun in this respect.

But, in the THIRD *place, the sun has a* GREAT COMFORTING POWER; and for this reason, too, Jesus is like it.

Solomon says: 'Truly the light is sweet, and a *pleasant thing it is for the eyes to behold the sun.*' (Ecclesiastes ii. 7.) But we who see the sun every day hardly know how to value it. We cannot tell what a great blessing we have in his pleasant light, and what a comfort his bright beams are to us! But if we were obliged to live for a while where we could have no sunshine, or even sunlight, then when we saw the light of the sun and his beautiful beams once more, we should understand what a comforting power the sun has.

Up in the arctic region, near the North Pole, you know there is a long night of six months every year, in which the sun is never seen. Our brave townsman, Dr. Kane, spent two winters there some years ago. He went with his little band of heroes in the hope of finding out something about the fate of Sir John Franklin and his noble company, who had perished there some years before. Well, if we had been six months without seeing the sun, as Dr. Kane was, we should then understand what a comforting thing it is to see the sun. I have just been looking at Dr. Kane's book to see what he says about his feelings on seeing the sun after those long, dark nights.

On the first occasion, after the six dark months were over, when the doctor knew that the sun was coming back, he climbed up the peak of a mountain to catch the first view of his returning beams. 'Then,' he says, '*I nestled in the sunshine. I felt as if I was bathing in perfumed water.*' Only think of taking a bath in Cologne-water or rose-water! What a comfortable feeling it would give you! That was just how Dr. Kane felt when he took his first sunshine bath, after he had been so long without seeing the sun.

The next year, when he first saw the sun again after the long winter, his feelings of gladness broke out in these words : '*Blessed be the great Author of light! To-day I have once more looked upon the sun.*' Looking at the sun, he said, seemed like an act of worship. It made that day seem like Sunday to him. Think of Dr. Kane, alone, on that mountain peak, with nothing but ice and snow around him, standing there to gaze once more upon the sun! Ah! he was feeling then, all through his soul, what a great power to comfort the sun has.

Some years ago, a good minister of Jesus was visiting among the poor in a city in Scotland. One day he stepped into a hovel. It was dimly lighted by a single window of four small panes of glass. There was very little furniture in it, but everything was very neat and clean. An aged Christian woman lived in that humble dwelling. She was in very feeble health, and almost blind. The minister saw her sitting in the corner, by the fire. He went and sat down by her, and began to talk with her. He found that, although she lived there alone, in much poverty and suffering, she was yet very happy. 'How do you manage to spend your long days here, all alone ?' asked the minister.

'I am not alone,' she said, 'because Jesus is with me; and thinking about Him makes the time pass pleasantly.

My neighbours are kind, and when they come in to help me I love to talk to them about Jesus. But there is one hour in the day which is the most pleasant of all to me. Do you see that little window?' she asked, pointing across the room. 'For about an hour every day, when it is not cloudy, the sun shines in there. Then I take my large printed Bible, and sit down in the sunshine, where I can see well enough to read. And O, Sir, *that is a blessed hour to me!*'

What power the sun had to comfort that poor woman! And when his bright light began to shine through that little window, it must have seemed as if an angel from heaven had come in there, and was shaking down blessings from his golden wings. And oh, how many poor creatures there are all over the earth who feel, when the bright sun comes pouring in his blessed light on them, that he has great power to comfort!

And Jesus is just like the sun in this respect. When we learn to love Jesus, hearing and reading and thinking about Him has the same effect upon the soul that sunshine has on the body. It has power to gladden or to comfort. Let me give you one or two illustrations of the way in which Jesus does this.

A little boy was trying to amuse himself once in his mother's sick chamber. To do this without making a noise, he got a pencil and paper, and began printing his name. Presently he made a mistake; and, wetting his finger, he tried to rub it out, as he used to do with his slate. His mother saw what he was doing. She called him to her, and said: 'My son, you can't rub those marks out with your fingers. There is only one thing that will rub them out, and that is a piece of india-rubber. But do you know that God writes down all you do in a book? Every bad word and act and thought and feeling is written down there; and do you think, my dear boy, you can ever rub out those marks against you?'

The little fellow had never thought of this before. His face grew red and then pale. He was very much distressed to think of those dreadful marks against him in God's book. He went away by himself for a while. Then he came back, and going up to his mother's bedside he said, ' Dear mother, can't the blood of Jesus rub out the mark of my sins from God's book?'

' Yes, my dear child,' said his mother. ' That's the way, the only way in which our sins can be blotted out.' Then the little fellow wiped away the tears that had filled his eyes, and felt happy. That sweet verse came to his mind like a beam of light from the Sun of Righteousness, and it had power to comfort him.

I was reading lately about a man who had once been a member of the Church, but who fell into sin, and gave up going to church. He even ceased to believe the Bible, and became an infidel. But at last he was taken sick, and felt that he was going to die. He thought of his sins, and was greatly alarmed. He was in such distress that it was fearful to see him. He trembled so that the bed on which he was lying fairly shook under him. They tried to get a minister to go and see him; but there was not one in the neighbourhood where he lived. It happened that a young man who was a Christian was on a visit to a family living near. He was asked to go and see the sick man. He went. He sat down by his bed-side. But when he saw the great agony the poor man was in, he knew not what to say. He asked him what caused him so much distress.

' My sins! my sins!' was his depairing cry. The young man was afraid to speak any words of his own : so he repeated a number of passages of Scripture which

came into his mind, and which he thought would suit
the poor man's case. Among these texts was this:
'This is a faithful saying, and worthy of all acceptation,
that Christ Jesus came into the world to save sinners.'
(1 Timothy i. 15.) The man caught at this text in a
moment. It seemed to take right hold of his mind.
'Repeat that text,' he said to the young man. It was
repeated. 'Is that true?' he asked. 'It is,' was the
answer; 'it is God's own truth,—the word of Him who
cannot lie.' 'Then I am safe,' said the sick man. The
look of horror passed away from his face, and the smile
of peace took its place. The change was effected in a
moment. It was wonderful. It was like the voice of
Jesus when He rebuked the stormy sea, 'and the wind
ceased, and immediately there was a great calm.' It
was like a sudden burst of sunshine coming into a dark
room and filling it with brightness. That one text of
Scripture was like a beam from the Sun of Righteousness, and there was great power to comfort in it.

And thus we see that there are three reasons why
Jesus is like the sun. These refer to the different
kinds of power which the sun exercises, and in which
Jesus resembles it. These are,—a *great drawing power;*
a *great healing power;* and a *great comforting power.*

Now, before closing, let me say to you, my dear
young friends, that there are *two* things we ought to do
with this light which comes to us from the Sun of
Righteousness. One is this—*We ought to use it ourselves.*
God gives us the light of day, in order that we may see
how to do the work we have to do. And then He
expects us to do it. And God gives us the light of the
Sun of Righteousness to show us how to become Christians. And when this light is shining about us, God
expects us to become Christians. And if we are really
trying to love and serve Jesus, then we are using this

light for ourselves. This is just what Jesus means, when He says, 'While ye have the light, walk in the light, that ye may be the children of the light.'

The other thing we ought to do with this light is—*To share it with others.* There are many ways in which we may do this. One of these is by helping to send the gospel to those who are without it. When we help to establish Sunday-schools where there are none; when we give libraries and good books to poor schools; and when we do what we can to send Bibles and missionaries to the heathen,—then we are sharing our light with others. Let us do all we can in these ways, because Jesus loves to have us do these things, and because doing them will make us useful and happy.

II.

JESUS THE LIGHT OF THE WORLD.

'I am the light of the world.'—JOHN viii. 12.

WE are speaking of 'rays from the Sun of Righteousness.' We have tried to show that Jesus is Himself the Sun of Righteousness. It is proper to speak about a tree before speaking of the fruit that grows upon it. It is proper to speak about a fountain before speaking of the streams that flow from it. And so it is proper to speak about the sun before speaking of the rays that shine from it. All the light that comes to us from the sun is made up of the rays, or beams, which he is pouring forth continually. When this light is decomposed, or taken to pieces, it is found to be made up of seven different coloured rays. There are blue, and red, and orange, and yellow, and so on. These rays differ from each other in other things as much as they do in colour. The red ray has more heat in it than any of the others. The yellow is the coldest of all the rays ; and the violet is the quickest in its motion. And if we wish to have a proper understanding of the light which comes from the sun, we must find out all we can about the different rays that make up this light.

And so if we would have a right knowledge of Jesus, if we would understand what a glorious Saviour He is, we must study the different rays that shine from Him as

the Sun of Righteousness. These rays are the names,
or titles, given to Jesus in the Bible. And this is what
we shall try to do in these sermons. We shall take up
different parts of the character of Jesus, and the work
that He does for His people, and talk about them. And
when we get through, I hope we shall find that we
understand more about Jesus as the Saviour of our
souls, and as our friend and brother, than we have ever
known before.

'I am the light of the world.'

This was what Jesus said of Himself. When He
spoke these words, it was early in the morning. He
had just come from the Mount of Olives. As He
approached the temple, it may have been that the sun
burst out, and poured a flood of light over all that
beautiful building. Its marble walls and golden spires
were glittering in the beams of the sun. And as the
disciples were gazing in wonder at the beautiful sight,
Jesus pointed to that sun as an image, or figure, of Him
self. It was just as if He had said, 'Look at that sun
with the light it pours out, and then look at Me. I am
the light of the world. All that the light of yonder sun
is doing for the bodies of men I have come to do for
their souls.'

And in comparing Jesus to the light, I wish to
speak of *four* things for which we are dependent on the
light. These four things show us how necessary the
light is to us, and how well Jesus may be compared to
it, because we are dependent on Him for the very same
things for our souls.

And the FIRST *thing for which we are dependent on the
light is* LIFE.

The light of the sun has no power to make dead
things alive by shining upon them. Suppose we take

the dead body of a child, or of a man or woman; or suppose we take a dead plant or flower or tree, and lay it down where the light of the sun can shine on it: will this bring it back to life again? No. The light has no power to do that. It cannot *give* life when it does not exist; but it can help to preserve it, or keep it where it does exist. The light of the sun is needed in order to keep alive the grass and the plants, the flowers and the trees. And it is needed, too, to keep our bodies, and the bodies of all the animals, alive. If the light were taken away, all the trees of the forest would die. So would all the plants and flowers of the garden, and all the grass of the fields. All the animals in the world, and all the people too, would die, if it were not for the light. Light is necessary to preserve the life of our bodies, and the life of all things about us.

And for this reason Jesus might well say of Himself: 'I am the *light* of the world.' He is more necessary for the life of our souls than the light of the sun is for the life of our bodies. The light which shines from Jesus, and of which He speaks in our text, is made up of the truths taught us in the Bible about His character and work; or about what He is in Himself, and what He does for us. And this light is more important to our souls than the light of the sun is to our bodies. The light which shines from Jesus has the power of giving life to souls that are dead, as well as of keeping it when it is given.

When ministers preach the gospel, or when Christian people read it or teach it to others, they are scattering light from Jesus, the Sun of Righteousness. And the light thus scattered has the power of giving life to souls that are dead in sins. A single ray of this light sometimes gives life, when it seemed impossible to give it. Let us look at some illustrations of the way in which this is done.

C

In a certain part of England there is a village called Adwinkle. Many years ago, the Rev. Thomas Hawes, an earnest man of God, was the minister of the church in this village. At the time to which our story refers, the members of Mr. Hawes' church had a new organ built, so that they might have better music in connection with their worship. The organ was finished, and on a particular Sunday it was to be used for the first time. The choir had been practising a long time for that occasion. They had some beautiful pieces to sing, and there was to be a grand musical performance. The whole village was excited about it ; and people who were not in the habit of going to church were going on that day to hear the new organ.

There was a man living in Adwinkle then who kept the village inn, or tavern. He was a rough, drunken, swearing, wicked man. Of course *he* never went to church. He professed to be an infidel, and never read the Bible. But he was very fond of music. He wanted very much to go to church and hear the new organ. But he was not willing to listen to the minister while praying or reading the Bible, or preaching even for the pleasure of hearing the new organ. What could he do? After thinking over it a good while, he made up his mind that he would go to church and hear the organ, and as soon as the music was over would stop up his ears with his fingers, so as not to hear any of the service. He went accordingly. He heard the voluntary and the opening piece played. Then he stopped his ears while the minister was praying. He listened to the hymn after the prayer, and stopped his ears again while the minister was reading the Scriptures. But just in the midst of this part of the service there came a fly, and lighted on his big, red nose. He put out his under lip, and tried to send up a blast of air that would blow him off. But the fly held on. Then he shook his head again and again. The fly took no notice of it. He went deliberately crawling about over the drunkard's nose and face, and tickled him more than he could bear. At last he removed his right hand from his ear, for a moment, to drive the fly away. While doing this, he heard the minister read these words : ' *He that hath ears to hear, let him hear.*' They had such an effect upon him, that he went home, and began earnestly to read his Bible ; and in a short time he became a Christian.

Here you see how that one text was like a ray from the Sun of Righteousness. It brought the light of truth into that man's darkened mind. And that light was the life of his soul.

' One day,' said a minister in England, ' I was walking out near an encampment of gipsies. I went in among them. While buying some of the baskets they were making I heard that there was a sick boy in their camp. I begged that I might be allowed to go and see him. The father asked :—

' " Do you want to talk about religion to him ? "

' " No."

' " What then ? "

' " Only about Jesus."

' " Well, then, you may go; but mind, if you talk about religion, I 'll set the dog on you."

' In one of the tents I found the lad alone. He was sick with consumption, and very near his end. His eyes were closed, and he looked like one already dead. Very slowly in his ears I repeated this one text of Scripture : " God so loved the world, that He gave His only begotten Son, that whosoever believeth in Him should not perish, but have everlasting life.' I repeated this over five times. He seemed to take no notice. I could not tell that he even heard me. I repeated it the sixth time. Then he opened his eyes, and smiled. In a low whisper he said :—

' " And I never thanked Him ; but nobody never told me. I 'turn Him many thanks,—only a poor gipsy chap! I see, I see ! I thank Him kindly." '

The minister's heart was full as he kneeled down to offer a prayer over the poor boy. He saw his lips move again. He leaned down to listen. He caught,—' That 's it.' There were other words, but he could not understand.

On calling the next day, he found the poor boy was gone. His father said he had been very ' peaceable,' and had ' a nice, tidy death.'

Now when that minister was repeating, again and again, the words of that sweet text to the poor gipsy boy, telling him ' the old, old story,' and telling it to him ' simply ' and ' slowly,' ' that he might take it in,' he was holding a beam from ' the Light of the world,' a ray from the Sun of Righteousness, and pouring it on the darkness of a poor dying soul. And that one ray of light brought life to that soul. Jesus may well be called ' the Light of the world,' because we are dependent on this light for *life*.

But we are dependent on light for GROWTH, *as well as life; and this is the* SECOND *reason why Jesus may be compared to the light.*

All the growth that takes place in plants and trees depends on the light. If the light were taken away from them, and they were kept in the dark, they would not grow. We may find an illustration of this in most of our cellars. Suppose you have a lot of potatoes in your cellar. If there is no window in the cellar, and no light gets in, the potatoes, if left there long enough, will rot and spoil; but they will not grow. But if there is a window on the other side of the cellar, and a little light finds its way in there, it will have a strange effect upon those potatoes. Instead of rotting, they will begin to grow. Their eyes will swell up, and little sprouts will shoot out from them. These sprouts will grow over towards the window. As you see them straggling across the cellar floor, it looks as if the potatoes were stretching out their arms towards the light, and begging it to come and help them to grow. And that is just what the potatoes want. They wish to get more light to help them grow.

And it is the same with the flowers and the trees, and with every other kind of vegetable. Each, in its place, is dependent on the light. None of them can grow without it. Here is an acorn. What a tiny little thing it is! Yet there is a big oak-tree stowed away in this little cup. But then that tree can never get out of the acorn and grow up to its proper size without the help of the sunlight. It needs the light to make it begin to grow. Then it springs up a tender little sprouting thing, which an infant's foot could crush. But every year it grows higher and broader and stronger. And as it goes on increasing in size and strength, the trunk depends on the branches, and the branches depend on the leaves, and the leaves depend on the sunlight for all they need to make the tree grow.

And just in the same way our souls depend for their growth on the light that Jesus gives. A young Christian, just converted, is like an acorn just beginning to grow. A mature Christian, who has reached what the Apostle Paul calls 'the stature of a perfect man in Christ,' is like the tree that has grown up to its full size out of the little acorn. The tree can only grow by the help of the light which the sun gives, and the soul can only grow by the help of the light which Jesus gives. And this is one reason why Jesus says of Him-self, 'I am the Light of the world.'

Here is a story about a beggar boy who was changed into a Christian gentleman. When he was a beggar boy, he was like the acorn that had the oak-tree hid away inside of it. When he became a Christian gentle-man, he was like the great oak-tree that had grown up out of its acorn. And it was the light which Jesus gives that made this oak-tree of a Christian gentleman grow out of that acorn of a beggar boy.

A New York merchant, who is a Sunday-school teacher, was called upon for a speech at a great Sunday-school meeting out in the West. He said: 'I 'll tell you a little story of a beggar boy. I started out one fine Sunday morning to get up some recruits for my class. At the corner of the street I met a barefooted boy, without hat or coat. His hair was fiery red, and looked as if it had never been combed. I asked the boy if he would come to school. " No, Sir ! " was his sharp reply.

' " You ought to go to Sunday-school," I said kindly.

' " What for ? " he asked.

' " We teach boys to be good," I said.

' " But I don't want to be good," he said.

' " Why not want to be good ? " I asked earnestly.

' " Because I am hungry," was his quick reply.

' " It is now nine o'clock," I said, looking at my watch ; " haven't you had any breakfast yet ? "

' " No, Sir."

' " Where do you live ? "

' " Up the alley there, with aunty ; she 's sick."

' " Will you eat some gingerbread and crackers if I go and get some ? "

' " Yes, Sir, that I will ; and be glad to get 'em."

'I brought a lot, and set them before him. He ate them in a way which showed how keenly hungry he was. I asked him if he would like some more. "A little more, if you please, Sir," said the boy.

'I got a fresh supply, and set them before him. I waited till he had done eating; then I said: "My boy, will you go with me to school now?"

'"You've been so kind to me, Sir," said he, "I'll go anywhere with you. Please wait till I take what's left of the gingerbread round to aunty, and then I'll go with you."

'He returned directly to the place where I was waiting for him, and went with me to school.

'He had never been to school before. He thought of school as a place where boys had to hold out their hands to be slapped with a ruler, and have their hair pulled, and their ears pinched. But when he found himself in the hands of a pleasant-looking young lady, who treated him kindly, and said nothing about his shabby clothes, he was greatly surprised.

'He became a regular attendant. He told all the boys of his acquaintance about the school, and persuaded many of them to attend. About two years after this a lot of boys from New York were sent out West, and distributed among the farmers. My red-haired boy was sent among them. I used to hear of him for a while, that he was getting on and doing well. I have lost sight of him for years now, but I have no doubt he is doing good wherever he is.' The gentleman then said a few words about the importance of getting the poor and neglected children of our large cities into Sunday-schools, and then sat down.

In a moment, a tall, good-looking gentleman, with red hair, stood up in the meeting, and said: 'Ladies and gentlemen, I am the red-haired beggar boy of New

York who ate that gentleman's gingerbread. I have lived in the West for years, and been prospered. I am now a rich man. I own five hundred acres of as good land as the sun shines on. My horses and carriage are at the door; and when the meeting is over I shall be happy to take my old friend to my home, where he will be welcome to stay as long as he pleases. I am a member of a Church, and the superintendent of a Sabbath-school; and I owe all that I have in *this* world, and all that I hope for in the next, to what was taught me about Jesus in the Sabbath-school!'

Now the growth of a great oak-tree from a little acorn is not at all more wonderful than the change which took place when that little, hungry, ignorant, beggar boy was turned into that intelligent Christian gentleman. And yet it was all brought about by the light which Jesus gives.

The second thing for which we are dependent on light is *growth;* and this is a good reason why Jesus may be compared to light.

But the THIRD *thing for which we are dependent on light is* BEAUTY.

Light is one of the most beautiful things that God has made. It is beautiful in itself, and it makes other things beautiful. All the beauty that we see in the world around us we owe to the light. Suppose you go into a garden full of beautiful flowers on a dark night. How many colours will you see among all the flowers? Only one. And what colour will that be? Black. Suppose you go and look at a gallery of beautiful paintings in the dark. How many colours will you see? Only one. And that will be what? Black. You must have light to bring out to view all the different colours of the flowers in the garden, or the pictures in the gallery. Suppose you look at a great mass of clouds in the western sky at the close of the afternoon. They are all of one colour; and this is a dark grey, almost black. There is very little beauty in those clouds. When you have seen them once, you do not care to see them again. But presently the sun gets behind them. He pours a flood of light over them and through them; and what a change takes place in a moment! They look now as if they had been bathed in liquid gold. How they glow and sparkle! What different colours are there! There is white, and grey, and yellow, and blue, and purple. They are changing all the while, and mingling one with another. How beautiful they are! And what has made this change? The light has done it. All those beautiful colours are made by the light.

And Jesus may well be called 'the light of the world' on this account. Like the light, He is beautiful in Himself, and He makes others beautiful. Jesus is a glorious sun,—'the Sun of Righteousness.' And the light that He gives comes to us like sunbeams, that spread brightness and beauty everywhere.

And the most interesting thing about this light is that it has the power of making *us* beautiful, if we use it properly. We sometimes hear of persons putting powder and paint on their faces, to make them look beautiful. But if we use the light which Jesus gives, that is, if we become true Christians, and try to be like Jesus, this will make us more beautiful than anything else. You know that a sculptor is one whose business it is to make statues, or figures of men in marble. He will set before him a beautiful model of the head and face of a man, and then try to make one like it. He will take a block of marble, and hew it out into the shape of a man. At first it will be rough, and not much like the model. But with his chisel in one hand,

and his mallet in the other, he keeps working away at it. It cannot be done at once, but requires great patience and perseverance. He chips off a little piece here, and a little piece there. Now he does something to the chin, and now to the cheek, and now to the nose, and now to the lips. He goes over it again and again. He looks first at the model, and then at his own work, and tries to make this just like that. And every Christian is a kind of sculptor; only, instead of working in marble, he is working in mind or spirit. He sets Jesus before him as his model, and tries to make his own soul like that of Jesus. And when we look to Jesus, and ask ourselves, What would *He* do, or say, or think, if He were in our place? and then try to do, or think, or feel, or say, just as he would, why, then, we are growing like Jesus. And there is nothing in the world that will make us look so beautiful as this. We sometimes see persons who were beautiful when young, but who become ugly as they grow older. But if we are growing like Jesus, and the light He gives is making us beautiful, then the longer we live, and the older we get, the more beautiful we shall grow.

There is living in the town of New Hartford, in Connecticut, in a small, unpainted house by the road-side, about two miles from the village, a poor woman by the name of Chloe Lankton. She is confined to her bed with a disease that never can be cured in this life. For more than thirty years she has lain on that humble bed unable to rise or be removed. She is in constant bodily pain. At times her sufferings are so great that it is wonderful how she can live. Her father and mother and four sisters have died, one after another, and been carried from her sight, since she has lain on that bed. She has no relative in the world, and no support but what friends give without being asked. She has no one to wait on her but a hired servant. Yet the light which Jesus gives has so shined into the heart of that lonely sufferer as to make her look really beautiful. Her face is said to beam almost like the face of an angel. Those who go to see her come away charmed, as if they had been to visit a princess. Young people, for miles around, go to see her; not from pity, but for the pleasure they find in her company. The very children go in troops to her house to show her all their treasures, and ask her advice about all their plans and playthings. And what has given this poor, lonely sufferer such power to please and charm both old and young? Nothing but the light which Jesus gives. This shines into her heart. It makes her gentle and loving and kind as he is. It gives to her voice and face and manner a sweetness and beauty that cause all who know her to love her. The light gives beauty, and for this reason Jesus may be compared to the light.

But there is a FOURTH *thing for which we are dependent on the light; viz.,* SAFETY. And on this account Jesus may be compared to the light.

There is danger in darkness. We cannot see the evils that threaten us then, nor how to escape them. It is under the cover of darkness that thieves go forth to rob, and murderers to kill, and all sorts of wicked people to do bad things. And it was the knowledge He had of this which led our Saviour to say : 'He that doeth evil hateth the light, neither cometh to the light, lest his deeds should be reproved.' (John iii. 20.) Our merchants and shop-keepers have found out that there is safety in light; and they are putting this knowledge to a good use.

When I was a boy, I remember that at night the jewellers' shops, and others that had valuable things in

them, used to have heavy wooden or iron shutters to
the windows; and these would be fastened with locks
or great iron bolts and bars. And all this was done
for safety. But now many of those shops have no
shutters at all to them; and others only have a thin wire
grating over them. But if you stop and look through
one of those windows at night, you will find that the
gas is lighted in the shop, and kept burning. If a
thief should get in there and begin to steal, he would be
seen by the watchman or the people going by. And so
the thieves stay away. They are afraid to go into a
shop where the gas is burning. This shows us that
there is safety in light.

And Jesus may well be called 'the Light of the
world,' because He brings salvation wherever He comes.
And salvation means *safety*. When we learn to know
Him, and trust in Him, we are safe. Solomon says:
'The name of the Lord is a strong tower; the righteous runneth into it, and is safe." (Proverbs xviii.
10.) And when David is speaking of the way in which
God takes care of His people, he says: 'He shall defend
thee under His wings, and thou shalt be safe under His
feathers; His faithfulness and truth shall be thy shield
and buckler." (Psalm xci. 4, Prayer-book version.) Here
God compares Himself to a bird that takes its little
ones under its wings for safety. This is what Jesus
said He wanted to do for the Jews, and they would
not let Him. (Matthew xxiii. 37.) But He does this for
all who love Him. When we learn to know Him and
trust Him, it is just as if a beam of light had shone
down on our path to show us the way to a safe hiding-
place.

Not long ago a railway train was going over the
Alleghany Mountains. It had reached a place where
there was a deep precipice on one side, and a steep wall

of solid rock that rose sheer up to a great height on the
other. The cars were running along quite close to this
rocky wall. All at once the whistle screamed the signal,
' Down brakes! down brakes! '

The passengers were alarmed. They raised the
windows and looked out, expecting to see or hear of
some dreadful disaster. The engineer had discovered
a little girl and her young brother playing upon the
track, just a little way in front of the engine. It was
impossible to stop the train in time, and it seemed as if
the poor children must be crushed to death. But just
at this moment the girl's eye caught sight of two niches
in the wall of rock, made by blasting. Snatching up
her little brother, she pressed him into one of these
niches, and put herself in the other. And while the
long train went by, the passengers heard the voice of
the little girl saying : ' Cling close to the rock, Johnny!
cling close to the rock! '

How beautiful this was! And it shows us how
Jesus makes His people safe. We are exposed to
dangers worse than those which threatened this little
girl. But Jesus sheds the light of His truth on our path.
This shows us that He is the Rock in which we may
find a hiding-place. And when we look up to Him and
say :—

> ' Rock of ages, cleft for me,
> Let me hide myself in Thee ;'

then, like this little girl, we are ' clinging close to the
rock.' And the safety which we find in doing this is
safety found in the light which Jesus gives.

I remember hearing of a tree somewhere in the East
Indies, which illustrates very sweetly this part of our
subject. This tree is what is called a non-conductor of
lightning. This means that the tree has some strange

power in it, which prevents the lightning from striking
it. They have dreadful thunderstorms in that country.
And when those storms burst, the thunder roars,
and the lightning flashes out, and strikes other trees
in the neighbourhood; but it never touches this
tree.

The people in the neighbourhood know this. And
when they see the storm gathering, they leave their
houses, and get under the shelter of this tree for
safety. And they always find it there. No matter
how loud the thunder or how sharp the lightning, they
are safe under that tree. The lightning never strikes
that tree; and nobody under the shadow of it is ever
hurt.

What a beautiful illustration this is of the tree of
Calvary, the cross on which Jesus died for us! The
Bible tells us of 'the wrath to come.' This will be the
storm of God's anger against sinners. It will be dreadful when that storm bursts. But the lightning of God's
wrath will never strike the Tree of Calvary,—the Cross
on which Jesus died. All who are under the shadow of
this tree will be safe. Jesus sheds the light of His
gospel around us, in order to show us the way to this
tree. And Jesus may well be called ' the light of the
world,' because there is safety in the light He gives.

And so we see there are four things for which we
are dependent on the light.

These are *life*, and *growth*, and *beauty*, and *safety*.
And as the light of the natural sun brings these four
blessings to our bodies, so the light which Jesus, the
Sun of Righteousness, gives secures the same sort of
blessings to our souls.

Let us be thankful that we have this light. ' And
while we have the light, let us walk in the light, that
we may be children of the light.' I pray God that each

of you, my dear young friends, may be able to say, as Bonar says in one of his sweet hymns :—

> 'I heard the voice of Jesus say :
>   I am this dark world's light ;
> Look unto Me ; thy morn shall rise,
>   And all thy day be bright.
> I came to Jesus, and I found
>   In Him my Star, my Sun ;
> And in that light of life I 'll walk
>   Till travelling days are done.'

'I AM THE LIGHT OF THE WORLD.'

'THE STARS, AS THEY SHINE CALMLY OUT IN THE SKY AT NIGHT,
ARE A GREAT HELP TO THEM IN STEERING THEIR VESSELS.'—
See page 50.

III.

THE BRIGHT AND MORNING STAR.

'I am the bright and morning star.'—REVELATION xxii. 16.

THIS is one of the beautiful titles which Jesus applies to Himself. And among them all there is none more delightful than this. We have already spoken of Him as 'the Sun of Righteousness' and as 'the Light of the world.' And now the *star* comes in very sweetly, as another of those bright and beautiful things that remind us of our blessed Saviour whenever we see them. We may well consider this as one of the *'Rays from the Sun of Righteousness.'*

Jesus was often spoken of as a star before He came into our world. And when He was born, we remember that wonderful star which appeared to 'the wise men in the east,' to tell them that the great King of the Jews had come, and afterwards to guide them to the stable in Bethlehem where Jesus lay.

All the stars are very beautiful to look at. But if we get up before daylight in the morning, and look out towards the east, where 'the bright and morning star' is shining, we shall see that *this* is more beautiful than the others. How clearly it stands out in the dark sky! With what soft and silvery light it shines! And as we stand gazing at it, we cannot help thinking how well

D

it may remind us of Jesus.   He said of Himself, ' I am
the bright and morning star.'

Jesus made use of a great many objects in the world
around us, in order to teach us what He is, and what
He does for us.   The vine, the rock, the tree, the fountain, the sun, the light, the star, are all used in this
way, either by Himself or by the ' holy men of old '
whom He employed to write the Bible.   And when He
does this, it is worth our while to study these different
objects ; for if we do so, we shall always find something
in each of them that will help us to understand the
character of Jesus and His work.   Now our subject is
' the bright and morning star.'

And the question for us to consider is this : when
we think of this beautiful star, what is there in it, or in
what it does, that should remind us of Jesus, and show
us how well He may be compared to such a star ?
There are *three* things which the star gives us, and for
which Jesus may well be compared to it.

In the FIRST *place, the star gives us* GUIDANCE.

Our sailors understand this better than any other
people.   When they are out at sea, far away from land,
the stars, as they shine calmly out in the sky at night,
are a great help to them in steering their vessels.
Most of the stars are changing their places all the
time.   These are not of so much use.   But there is *one*
star, especially, that is fixed.   It never changes its place.
In winter and in summer, it is always in just the same spot
in the heavens.   It will be there to-night.   It was there
when our Saviour was on earth, almost two thousand
years ago.   And a thousand years before that, when
David, the shepherd of Bethlehem, used to watch the
stars as he kept guard over his flocks by night, that
star was just in the same place where we can see it now.

But this star, the North Star, or the Pole Star, as we call it, is not a very bright star. It can only be seen when the sky is clear. And so, to help the sailor find out about where this Pole Star is, when he cannot see it, God has put two very bright stars in the sky, not far from the Pole Star. These two stars belong to a group of stars known as *the Great Bear*. Get some one to show them to you, and then you will always know them. They can be seen every clear night. Two of the stars in this group are called ' *the pointers*,' because a line drawn through them and continued on will touch the North Star. Thus they seem all the while to be *pointing* to it. And so, if the sailor cannot see the North Star itself, yet, when he sees these pointers, he knows just where to look for the North Star. And when he knows where that star is, it gives him guidance. He knows then how to steer his vessel, in order to reach the port for which he is sailing.

Now this life is like an ocean ; and we are all like ships sailing across the ocean. We are out of sight of land. We cannot see that heavenly harbour which we desire to reach at last. And there is nothing that we need so much as guidance. We know not how to steer our vessel so as to be able to reach that blessed harbour. And one reason why Jesus is called ' the bright and morning star ' is because He shows us the way to heaven, and guides us in that way.

There are rocks and shoals in the sailor's way, and he needs guidance to enable him to steer clear of them, and keep from being wrecked. And in trying to make our way to heaven, the sins and temptations around us are the rocks and shoals we meet with ; and if we look to Jesus as our star, He will guide us, so that we can steer clear of these dangers. It is mainly through the Bible that Jesus, our bright and morning star, gives us

D 2

the guidance that we need. If we read it carefully, and *follow* its teachings, it will help us to escape a great many dangers, and keep us safe from a great many troubles.

I saw a good story lately, that was headed

HOW TO ESCAPE THE TRAP.

It is a sort of fable. The story says that a company of rats once met in the cellar of a house, to consult together about their safety. A large steel trap had been set in that cellar. It was baited with a good big piece of cheese, which smelt very nice, and which they wanted very much to get at. But they had seen a number of their friends killed and wounded by this trap. In this way they had learned that it was a dangerous thing to meddle with. And now they had met together to see if they could not find out some way of getting that nice cheese out of the trap, without any injury to themselves. Many long speeches were made, and many plans suggested ; but none of them seemed to answer. At last one of them got up, and said : ' I move that a committee of two of the strongest among us be appointed to attend to this business. And I think if one of the committee will put his paws upon the spring and keep it down, then the other can take away the cheese with safety.' This seemed to meet with great favour. They agreed that this was the best plan that had been suggested, and they uttered a loud squeal in favour of it.

But just then they were startled by a faint voice, and a poor lame rat, with only three legs, came limping into the meeting. He stood up to speak, and said : ' My friends, I have tried the plan that has just been proposed, and you see the result. I lost my leg by it

That is what it cost me. Now let me give you my advice. If you want to escape the dangers of that trap, the best way is to *let it alone*. *Don't touch it*. *Don't go near it*.

And this is one of the ways in which Jesus, our guiding star, keeps us out of danger. Every sin is like a trap. We cannot go near it without danger. And the advice which Jesus gives us, when we are tempted to any kind of sin, is always the same. He says : ' Let it alone. Flee from it. Have nothing to do with it.' The best way to escape the trap is not to go near it.

And then this ' bright and morning star ' shines upon us, to show us how we may find peace and safety for our souls, as well as to avoid the traps which Satan sets for us. Some years ago, there was a young man in England who was studying for the ministry, and who died before he got through with his studies. He wrote, however, a very sweet hymn about Jesus as ' The Star of Bethlehem.' He compared himself to a vessel at sea, in the midst of a dark and stormy night. He knew there was a harbour near, but he could not tell how to steer his way into it. The wind was tossing his vessel about. The waves were breaking over it; and it was just on the point of sinking.

> ' When suddenly a star appeared,
> It was the Star of Bethlehem.'

And then he goes on in that sweet hymn to tell what that star did for him. He says :

> ' It was my guide, my light, my all ;
> It bade my dark forebodings cease ;
> And through the storm and danger's thrall,
> It led me to the port of peace.'

And then he tells of the happiness that came to him

from following the guidance of this blessed Star, comparing his soul to a vessel that was safely anchored in a quiet harbour.

> 'Now safely moored, my perils o'er,
> I'll sing first night's diadem,
> For ever and for ever more
> The star—the star of Bethlehem.'

And what this beautiful star did for Henry Kirke White—this was the young man's name—it has done for multitudes besides. And it will do the same for you and me, if we follow it. It will 'guide our feet into the way of peace.' It will bring us to Jesus Himself. It will teach us to know Him and love Him and trust in Him. And when we learn to trust in Him, we shall find pardon and salvation and every blessing that we need in Him.

Jesus says : 'I a.. the bright and morning star.' The star gives GUIDANCE, and this is the FIRST reason why Jesus may well be compared to a star.

But the SECOND *thing which a star gives is* HOPE.

And this is another good reason why Jesus may be compared to a star. Jesus calls Himself 'the bright and morning star,' because that star is made to shine on purpose to give us hope. The morning star is very beautiful to look at. It does not give a great deal of light. You cannot see to read by that star. But, as you look at it, it tells you that the night is almost gone. You know that the sun will soon rise and shine, and then there will be light enough for everything. You will be able to see the fields and the woods and the beautiful flowers, and all the glorious things that God has made. That morning star gives us the hope that the darkness will soon be gone, and the light of day

be shining all about us. And Jesus may well be compared to such a star, because when He rises and shines
on our hearts He fills them with the sweet hope that
the darkness of this world will soon pass away, and the
bright, clear light of heaven will be shining around us.
And this hope is a bright and beautiful thing. It is
able to make us happy, when nothing else in the world
can do so.

Let me try to show you what a blessed thing this
hope is which Jesus gives to those who know and love
Him.

LIGHT IN A MINE.

There was a little boy in England named Willie,
whose parents were miners. They lived in a little cottage near the entrance of the mine; but their young son
had to stay down in the damp, dark mine all the week.
The only time when he came up out of the mine was
Saturday night. He always spent Sunday at home.
That was a bright and happy day to him. Then he
could see the green fields, and the trees, and the flowers,
and the beautiful sky, and bask in the bright beams of
the glorious sun. How he enjoyed those Sundays!
Everything seemed pleasant to him; but the Sunday-
school, to which he always went, was the pleasantest of
all. *There* he had learned to know Jesus as ' the bright
and morning star;' and we shall see directly what a
blessed hope this star gave him.

One day, while the miners were blasting, a stream of
water burst out. Pretty soon it began to fill up the
passage-way where they were working. They all fled
for life to the main shaft, or opening of the mine.
Among those who met here were the father and mother
of Willie, for they both worked in the mine. They
looked round for their little boy; but he was not there.

They called him : ' Willie ! O, Willie ! ' but there was
no answer. He worked in a little chamber in a far-off
part of the mine. His mother started to run for him.
But the narrow passage way was already filled with
water. Nobody could get through it. She found it
was impossible to reach her child. They were obliged
to go up, and leave their little boy behind, separated
from them by that flood of cold, dark water. Oh, how
hard this was ! But there was no help for it. Nobody
could get at poor Willie, in that dark and distant corner
of the mine, where he was shut up.

The great steam-pump was immediately set at work
to try and get out the water. It was kept going night
and day ; but it took several days before the water was
low enough to allow any one to enter the mine. Willie's
father was the first to enter. He knew where to look
for his boy. With a miner's lamp in his hand, he
waded through the passage, which was still half full of
water. Presently he came to the chamber where Willie
used to work. Here he held up his lamp and looked
round ; over there, stretched out on an upper ledge of
the coal, lay the body of poor Willie, cold and dead.
He had not been drowned, but had crept up there out of
the reach of the water, and had died a slow and linger-
ing death from the want of fresh air and food. The
poor, sorrowing father held up the lamp to let its light
fall on the face of his dear, dead boy. There was no
look of pain upon it. A sweet, happy smile seemed to
be resting on every feature, just as if he had been seeing
something beautiful, when he was dying all alone in
that dark corner of the mine. On looking a little
further, the father saw that Willie had died with his
pocket knife in his right hand. He wondered what
this meant. But he soon found out. Holding up his
lamp, and looking round him, he saw some letters cut

in the smooth surface of the wall of soft coal under which he had died. The letters were big and rough, for they had been cut in the dark, and the dear fellow had been obliged to feel his way with his fingers as well as he could. It took the poor father some time to spell them out, for his hand trembled so that he could hardly hold the lamp steady, and his eyes were so full of tears that it was hard work for him to see at all. But at last he managed to spell them out, and then he found that his dear boy had busied himself during his last hours in cutting this sweet text from the 27th Psalm in that rock of coal: ' *When my father and mother forsake me, then the Lord will take me up.*' How beautiful this was! Yes; Jesus, 'the bright and morning star,' was there, shining sweetly on that dear boy as he lay down to die in the corner of that dark mine! And the shining of this star gave him hope,—the hope of a bright and better home in heaven. And this blessed hope it was which left that sweet smile which the father saw on the face of his dear, dead boy.

Another story comes in very well here. It is not a true story, like the one we have just had, yet I use it because it illustrates very nicely what a blessed thing hope is. This story is about

THE GOOD ARAB.

The Arabs have a good many stories which are not true, but which are valuable because they illustrate important and useful lessons; and this is one of that kind.

A rich Arab was once travelling through a wilderness, when he was attacked by a band of robbers. They ordered him to give up everything he had, and threatened, with their drawn swords in their hands, to

kill him in a moment, if he hesitated. He ordered his
servants to give up all they had. They did so. Then
he handed over to the robbers three bags of gold which
were hidden away under the cloth of his saddle. He gave
them, too, a small cabinet of precious stones, which was
carefully stowed away with his other baggage. He also
delivered up his silver-hilted sword, with its ivory
sheath, and his splendid turban, made of blue silk, with
red tassels and sparkling with diamonds and other
jewels.

When he had done this, he said to the robbers :
'Now, masters, I have given you all I have. You are
welcome to them. Take them, and let me go.'

'Nay,' said the captain ; 'I can't let you go yet. I
see a silken cord hung round your neck. We must see
what is at the end of it before we part.'

The Arab calmly pulled this cord from his bosom.
At the end of it was a small phial, or glass bottle, that
seemed to be filled with water. Taking it in his hand,
he said,—

'I have given you freely everything else I had ; but
I cannot give you this. If I should give it to you, it
would be of no value to you, for you know not how to
use it. But it is worth all the world to me. I never
can part with it while I live.'

'Tell us,' said one of the robbers, 'why you give up
your gold and jewels, and set so much value on this
little phial !'

'This little phial,' said the good Arab, 'is the most
valuable thing in the world to me. When all my
worldly goods are taken away from me, and nothing is
left but the sandy shore and the barren wilderness, I
have only to put this little phial to my eye and look
through it, and immediately I see wonderful things.
The barren waste changes into a fertile field. Wells of

clear, cool water are bubbling up; refreshing streams are flowing through the beautiful plains; tall palm trees are spreading out their refreshing shade, and flowers in all their loveliness are blooming around me.'

'Let *me* look at this wonderful phial,' said the chief of the robbers, stepping up to the Arab. He handed it to the robber, who put it to his eyes and looked through it very earnestly, but it made no change in anything. The desert was desert, and the rocks were rocks still. Not a tree, or flower, or single beautiful thing appeared to him. He handed it back, and said, 'Why, I can't see anything through your phial.'

'That's just what I told you,' said the Arab. 'This phial was given to me by a prophet of God. It is the phial of hope. But no one can see the bright and beautiful things which it shows till they learn to know and love and serve God. Once I could see nothing more through this phial than you do now. But God has taught me how to use it; and now, whenever I look through it, everything is bright and beautiful. It always gives me comfort, and makes me happy. So I carry it round my neck. It is the greatest blessing that I have; and I would rather part with everything else I have in the world than part with this.'

Then the story says that the robbers gave back to the good Arab all the things they had taken away from him, and he went on his way feeling very happy. And this story affords a good illustration of the blessed hope which Jesus gives to those who love Him. This hope is just the same to us as if there were a door into heaven set open before us. We can look through that door whenever we are in trouble, and see all the blessed things that the Bible tells us of, and which God is preparing for His people. And Jesus may well be called

, the bright and morning star,' because he gives us HOPE.

But there is a THIRD *thing that Jesus gives, when we see Him as 'the bright and morning star,' and that is* JOY. And this is a good reason why Jesus may be compared to such a star.

One of our great poets has said, 'A thing of beauty is a *joy* for ever.' The meaning of this is, that it always makes people glad, or gives them joy, to see a beautiful thing. And this is true. Now a star is a beautiful thing. And 'the bright and morning star' is *very* beautiful. Whenever I think of this star, I am reminded of my first visit to Switzerland a good many years ago. We went up from Geneva to the Valley of Chamouni, to see Mont Blanc. It was Saturday evening when we arrived there. I wanted very much to see how that great mountain would look when the sun was rising on it. So, on the next morning, I got up between three and four o'clock to be in good time to see the sun rise. I dressed myself, and all alone walked quietly down the valley, that I might be ready to catch the first sight of the beams of the sun, as they began to shine upon the snowy summit of the mountain, and gild it with golden beauty. It was a beautifully clear night, or rather morning, though it was still quite dark. There was no mist around the mountain, and not a cloud in the sky. The summit of Mont Blanc is a great, rounded dome of snow. This was lifted far up into the clear, dark sky. And right over the top of the mountain I saw the morning star. How calm it seemed there! How soft and silvery was the light it shed! How brightly and beautifully it was shining down on the snowy summit of that great mountain. It was one of the most lovely sights I ever saw. I thought it was worth while to go all the way to Switzerland, if there had been nothing else to see there but just that beautiful sight of the morning star above the summit of Mont Blanc. As I walked slowly down the valley, looking at that beautiful star, I thought of these sweet words of Jesus, '*I am the bright and morning star.*' The sight of that star made me glad. It gave me joy then, while I was looking at it. And it gives me joy now, whenever I think about it.

But all the stars in the world put together are not half so beautiful as Jesus is. And when we see Him, and know Him, as 'our bright and morning star,' there is no joy to be found in anything else so great as that which He gives.

A star gives light; and we always connect the thought of joy and gladness with light. In the Bible, light and gladness are spoken of as though they were the same thing. Thus David says, 'Light is sown for the righteous, and *gladness* for the upright in heart.' (Psalm xcvii. 11.) And this is a proper way of speaking, because light is a joyous and a gladdening thing.

SINGING IN THE LIGHT.

Here is a story about a little boy in a mine, different from the one we had a short time ago, and which illustrates nicely this point of our subject. This little fellow lived far down in a deep, dark mine. He was stationed beside a door in a low passage-way, and his business was to open and shut that door when the cars came along, carrying the coal from one part of the mine to another. It was a dark and dismal place to be in; and yet that boy tried to make the best of it, and to be as cheerful and happy as he could under the circumstances. He built a little playhouse, with blocks of coal, in the corner of the mine where he had to stay. He would amuse himself by watching the miners as they were digging away at the coal. And when they threw aside the bits of candle which had burned too low for their use, he would pick them up, and lay them by in his playhouse.

One day a gentleman was visiting this mine. When he came to the place where this little boy was, he found him sitting down by his coal playhouse, and he stopped to have a little talk with him. He saw a lot of those bits of candles in front of his play-house.

'Well, my little man,' said he, 'pray, tell me what you are going to do with these bits of candles.'

' O, Sir,' said the cheerful boy, 'I saves 'em till I gets a big lot. Then I sticks 'em all over my playhouse, and lights 'em all at once; and then, while they 's burning, *I sits down in the light, and sings.*'

He was a wise little fellow. And if the dim light of those bits of candles could give that poor collier boy joy enough to set him a-singing in his gloomy corner of that dark mine, how happy and joyous we should be in the light which shines on us from Jesus, 'the bright and morning star' !

THE AFRICAN'S JOY IN JESUS.

A poor African had been brought to know Jesus, and to walk in the light which He causes to shine upon His people ; and this is the way in which he told of the joy which he found in Jesus.

'The story of Jesus,' said he, 'is my hymn, my prayer, my Bible. I weep tears of joy over it when I can't sing. And when I can't weep over it any longer, then I sing about it. I thank God for it, from the sole of my foot to the crown of my head.'

TALKING WITH JESUS.

A. good minister of the gospel was visiting among the poor, one winter's day, in a large city in Scotland.

He climbed up into a garret at the top of a very high house. He had been told that there was a poor old woman there, that nobody seemed to know about. He went on climbing up, till he found his way into that garret room. As he entered the room, he looked round. There was a bed, and a chair, and a table with a candle burning dimly on it, a very little fire on the hearth, and an old woman sitting by it with a large Testament on her lap.

The minister asked her what she was doing there. She said she was reading. 'Don't you feel lonely here?' he asked. 'Na, na,' was her reply. 'What do you do here all these long winter nights?'

'O,' she said, 'I just sit here, wi' me light, and wi' me fire, and wi' me New Testament on my knees, *talking wi' Jesus!*' This was very sweet. You see how pleasantly 'the bright and morning star' was shining in that poor old woman's garret room! And you see what joy she found in the beautiful light which that Star shed all through her lonely chamber! There is nothing else in all the world which could have given to that aged woman, in her poverty and loneliness, such comfort and joy as she found in having Jesus, 'the bright and morning star,' shedding down His blessed light upon her soul!

And thus we have seen three things that the star gives: they are *guidance*, and *hope*, and *joy*. And Jesus may well be called 'the bright and morning star,' because these are the very things that He gives to His people.

How thankful we should be that we have this beautiful Star to shine upon us! How anxious we should be to follow His guidance, and to have the hope and joy that He gives dwelling in our hearts, and making us cheerful and happy in our lives! Yes; and how earnestly we should pray, and labour too, to have this star arise and shine in all those parts of our world that are still full of darkness! We should look up to God and say, in the words of the hymn,—

'Let not Thy spreading Gospel rest
Till through the world Thy truth has run ;
Till with this Star all men are blessed,
Who see the light or feel the sun.'

'I AM THE BRIGHT AND MORNING STAR.'

'JUMPING TO HIS FEET HE STRETCHED OUT HIS HANDS TOWARDS
HEAVEN AND SHOUTED.'—*See page* 72.

IV.

JESUS THE SAVIOUR.

' Thou shalt call His name JESUS ; *for He shall save His people
from their sins.'*—MATTHEW i. 21.

THIS was what the angel Gabriel said to Joseph,
who afterwards married Mary, the mother of our
Saviour. When a baby is born, it is sometimes a good
while before his parents and friends can agree about his
name. But when our Saviour was born, there was no
difficulty in telling what He was to be called. It was all
arranged beforehand. God made choice of His name
in heaven, and sent an angel down to tell what that
name was to be. The angel said, ' Thou shalt call His
name—Jesus.' This is the sweetest name that ever was
given to any one. Some names sound very pleasantly
when we speak them, although they have no particular
meaning. But this name is sweet, not only because
it sounds pleasantly when we pronounce it,—Jesus,—
but also because it has so much meaning in it. The
angel said this name was given Him because He was to
' *save* His people from their sins.' The meaning of the
name Jesus is—*Saviour*. And what Jesus saves from
is sin.

Sin is the most dreadful thing in the world. All
the sickness and sorrow, and pain and misery that we

see around us were caused by sin. Sin brought death
into the world. As we travel over the earth, we find
graves everywhere. It was sin that dug all these graves.
The dreadful storms that sweep over the earth; the
fearful pestilences that cut men down, as the scythe
mows down the grass; and the terrible earthquakes
that destroy thousands of lives in a moment,—all these
were caused by sin. All the angry quarrels and bloody
battles that have taken place among men have been
occasioned by sin. And if this were *all* that sin does
although this is dreadful enough, still it would not be
so very bad. If sin only ended in the grave, if it had
no power to follow us into the other world, then it
would not be such a dreadful thing after all, and we
should not have so much reason to be afraid of it. But
it is not so. Sin does *not* end in the grave. It *will*
follow us into the other world. Unless it be pardoned
here, in this life, it will follow us into eternity, and cling
to us there for ever.

The Bible tells us that God has a dreadful prison on
the other side of the grave. It is sometimes called hell,
sometimes 'the bottomless pit,' and sometimes 'the
lake of fire.' The fire there, God tells us, was 'prepared for the devil and his angels.' It was prepared for
them because they were the first sinners. How dreadful
it is to think of being shut up in that terrible place!
And yet the Bible tells us that 'the wicked shall be
turned into hell, and all the people that forget God.'
(Psalm ix. 17.) And this is just what sin would bring
us all to, if we had no Saviour. This is what makes a
Saviour so necessary. And when God sent His Son
into our world, He ordered that He should be called by
this name Jesus, because He was to save His people
from their sins. And when we hear or think of the
name of Jesus, we are reminded of the dreadful suffer-

ings from which He saves us. And this is one of the thoughts which make His name seem so sweet to us. This is the reason why we can say with so much truth,—

> 'There is no name so sweet on earth,
> No name so sweet in heaven,
> As that before His wondrous birth
> To Christ the Saviour given.

> 'We love to sing around our King,
> And hail Him blessèd Jesus ;
> For there 's no word ear ever heard
> So dear, so sweet, as Jesus.'

This sweet text may well be considered as one of the beautiful 'Rays from the Sun of Righteousness.' And as we look at Jesus in the light of this ray, we may see *three* great things in Him, which should encourage us to seek Him as our Saviour.

In the FIRST *place, there is* GREAT POWER *in Jesus;* and this is a good reason why we should desire to have Him for our Saviour.

We need a Saviour because we are sinners. We are born into this world with hearts that are sinful and need to be changed. And this is what makes it so necessary that He who undertakes to be our Saviour should have very great power. He must have power to change our sinful hearts, and make them good. He must have power to help us to do what is right, and to refuse to do what is wrong. He must have power over all the holy angels, to command them to wait upon us, and help to take care of us. He must have power over Satan and the wicked angels, to keep them from doing us any harm. He must have power over the sun, and the moon, and the stars ; over winds, and storms, and earthquakes; over kings and rulers, and men and women,—over everybody and everything, so as to be able to make all things work together for good to those who love Him. And this is just the power that Jesus has. He said Himself, when He was in this world : '*All power is given unto Me in heaven, and in earth.*' (Matthew xxviii. 18.) And this power is given unto Him, on purpose that He might be just such a Saviour as we need. He can do everything for us that it is necessary to have done.

Soldiers like to follow a captain who has more strength, or courage, or knowledge, or skill in fighting, than any one else. And this is a good reason why we should all try to have Jesus for our Saviour, because He has more power to help and save and bless us than any one else has.

There is a story told of one of the old saints, which illustrates this part of our subject very well. His name was St. Christopher. The story says that he was born in the Black Forest, in Germany, some hundreds of years ago. When he grew up to be a man, he was as big as a giant, and his strength was equal to his size. Because he was so strong, he resolved to make every one serve him, unless he could find some one who was stronger than himself. He heard of a great baron who was the strongest man in the world, and was not afraid of anybody. He went to this baron, and offered to engage in his service.

After serving him awhile, he found that the baron was very much afraid of the devil. Then he left the baron's service, and offered to serve the devil, because he was stronger than the baron, and was not afraid of any one. But by-and-by he found out that the devil was afraid of Jesus. And then the story says that he quitted the devil's service, and went and offered himself

to Jesus, as His servant. Jesus received him kindly,
and the giant served Him as long as he lived, for he
never found any one stronger than Jesus.

Jesus has shown His great power by what He has
done for us. He has done for us what no one else in
the world could have done. Let me try to show you
what I mean by this.

THE MAN THAT PAID.

Some time ago, a Christian lady was spending the
summer at the seaside. She used to go about and visit
the cottages in the neighbourhood. In one of these
she found a poor, half-witted boy, named Matt. He
could not tell one letter from another, and seemed
hardly to have sense enough to understand anything.
She felt interested in him, and often visited him in his
home, and walked with him in the fields and along the
shore, trying to teach him something about God, and
heaven, and his own soul.

Before the summer was over, she found that the
poor boy, somehow or other, had learned to know that
he was a sinner; and he was greatly distressed about
it. She saw that the only way to comfort him would
be to teach him about Jesus, who came to 'save His
people from their sins.' But how could she expect this
poor, feeble-minded boy to understand these great
things? She resolved to try. Taking his hand kindly
in hers, she said to him one day, ' My poor boy, I know
that you are a sinner. These sins are the debts you
owe to God. Now when one man owes a debt to
another man which he can't pay, he must be put in
prison for it. God has a prison too, called hell. But
though you cannot pay these debts to God, you need
not go to prison; for *God loves you, and does not wish you*

to go there. God has a dear Son, named Jesus, Whom He sent all the way from heaven on purpose to pay your debts, and so keep you from going to prison. He did this by suffering and dying on the cross for you. And so, you see, this God-man, Jesus, has paid all your debts; and you don't have to go to prison.'

Matt listened with his eyes and ears wide open, while the lady was talking to him; and then, with great earnestness, he said, ' Tell it me again; tell it me again!' She repeated what she had said. She told him over again ' the old, old story of Jesus and His love;' she told it to him slowly and simply, 'that he might take it in.' And God, by His blessed Spirit, helped him to take it in. He saw and understood the great love of Jesus in dying for his sins. This took away all his fear. His sorrow was turned to joy, and his poor, distressed heart was comforted. For a time he seemed to forget everything but God and His great love in Jesus Christ. One day, while his kind friend was talking to him about Jesus, as they sat by the sea-side, his heart seemed full of joy, and jumping to his feet he stretched out his hands towards heaven and shouted, ' God, and Man who paid the debt, *Matt says thank You, thank You!* '

From that time, Matt never lost the joy that he found in having Jesus for his Saviour. Not long after he was taken sick, and died; and the last words he was heard to speak before he died were, ' Man that paid the debt, do come and fetch poor Matt to live with Thee.

And if Jesus could pay the debt of sin for all His people, and could make such a poor child as Matt understand about it, then He must have very great power. And this is the first reason why we should desire to have Him for our Saviour.

But there is GREAT WILLINGNESS *in Jesus to save, as well as great power; and this is the* SECOND *reason why we should seek Him as our Saviour.*

Sometimes we meet with persons who have great power to help others, but who are not willing to do it. We hear at times of very rich people, whose money gives them a great deal of power to help the poor and suffering, but they are not willing to help them. We have heard, at times, of persons who have stood by, and seen some of their fellow-creatures in danger of death by drowning or by fire, and have been unwilling to help them, although they had the power to do so. We have heard of persons who have been condemned to death. They are led out to die, even though they have done nothing wrong. A cruel king looks on, and sees what is taking place. He has power to save their lives, if he chooses to do so. It only needs that he should write a line. Nay, he need not even take that trouble. He can do it, by just lifting his finger or nodding his head. Yet he is not willing to do even that. He has the power to save, but not the willingness.

But how different it is with Jesus! His willingness to save is just as great as His power. The Bible tells us that He is ' *abundant* in mercy! ' 'He is *ready* to forgive,' and 'He *waiteth* to be gracious.' He says Himself, ' Him that cometh unto Me *I will in no wise cast out*.' (John vi. 37.) He never refused to help or save any who came to Him when He was on earth. And He is just the same still. Whatever else you are not sure about, you may be *quite sure* of this,—that Jesus is always willing to save those who really want to be saved.

Let us look at some illustrations of the willingness of Jesus to save.

TAKE FREELY.

A ship was sailing once in the waters of the Southern Atlantic Ocean. The men on the look-out saw another vessel sailing up towards them. As she came nearer, they saw that she had signals of distress flying. They were wanting something. When they came near enough, the captain took his speaking trumpet, and hailed the stranger. 'Ship, ahoy!'

'What do you want?'

'We are dying for water: can you give us some?'

'Dip it up then. There is plenty around you. It's all fresh. You are off the mouth of the Amazon.'

The river Amazon, you know, is one of the widest and largest rivers in the world. It rolls a great volume of fresh water a hundred miles or more out to sea. The sailors on board that vessel were suffering and almost perishing for water to drink. They thought there was nothing but salt water about them, when they were surrounded for miles on every side by pure, fresh water. They had nothing to do but just to dip it up and drink.

And so Jesus is saying: 'If any man thirst, let him come unto *Me*, and drink.' (John vii. 37). The water of salvation is flowing all about us. 'The Spirit and the bride say, Come. And let him that heareth say, Come. And *whosoever will, let him come, and take of the water of life freely.*' Jesus is always willing to save everybody who wants to be saved.

A SAILOR'S EXPERIENCE.

A Swedish sailor attended the noon-day meeting in New York one day. When the meeting was opened, and any persons who wished to speak were invited to do so, the sailor stood up to say a few words. He was not in the habit of speaking in public, and he could not speak English very well; but he said he wanted to tell what Jesus had done for his soul.

'Once, on a long voyage,' said he, 'Jesus by His blessed Spirit showed me that I was a great sinner. Then my heart was full of sorrow: I said to myself, "What must I do to be saved?" But there was no one near to tell me what to do. I was thinking about my sins all the time, and was in great distress.

'One dark night I was standing at the wheel steering the ship, when I thought of Jesus. I tried to remember all that I had heard about Him, and lifted up my heart in prayer to Him for help. And all at once it seemed as if Jesus heard my prayer, and met me at the wheel. He spoke sweet words of love and mercy, as I stood at the wheel in the midst of that dark night. I heard Him whispering to me words like these: "Come to Me, weary, burdened one; I will give you rest. I cast none out who come to Me. I am meek and lowly of heart. Learn of Me. Take My yoke: it is easy. Take My burden: My grace will make it light."

'There at the wheel, in the dark and stormy night, Jesus came to me. He showed me how willing He is to receive poor sinners. I love Him because He first loved me. I cannot speak your language very well, but Jesus understands me, and I understand Him. And ever since I met Him at the wheel as the poor sinner's Friend, I want to tell everybody how willing Jesus is to save.'

SEEING I AM JESUS' LAMB.

An infant school, made up chiefly of Jewish children, was once put in the charge of a Christian lady. Among the hymns that she taught her scholars was a very sweet one beginning,—

'Seeing I am Jesus' lamb.'

Most of the scholars learned it in a short time, and they were very fond of singing it. One day in the middle of summer, one of the scholars met the teacher, and told her that, on the day before, a little Jewish boy belonging to the school had fallen into the river, and came very near being drowned.

On the next Sunday, this little fellow was in school again. The teacher spoke to him kindly, and asked him how it happened that he fell into the river.

He said he was walking on a plank by the edge of the river, when he stumbled, and fell into the water.

' Were you not very much frightened when you found yourself in the water ? '

' No, ma'am.'

' But what did you think about when the water closed over your head ? '

' Why,' said the little Israelite, and his eyes sparkled as he spoke, ' I thought over the words of the beautiful hymn you taught us :—

> ' Seeing I am Jesus' lamb,
>   He, I know, will lose me never ;
> When I stray, He seeketh me :
>   Death is but new life for ever.
> Father, to Thy home on high
> Take me, for Christ's lamb am I.'

This shows us that Jesus is just as willing to receive children, and to save them, as He is to save men and women. Indeed, when He was on earth He showed more interest in children than in any other persons. But Jesus is willing to receive, and save, and bless all kinds of persons ; and the more needy and helpless we are, the more ready He is to be our Friend and Saviour.

JUST AS I AM.

Here is an incident from the late war, which illustrates very sweetly how unwilling Jesus is to give any persons up, and how ready He always is to help and bless us.

A young man named James Rivers was engaged to be married to a young woman named Ellen Boone. The time for their wedding was not far off when the war broke out. Then the wedding was put off. James went to the war. For a while everything went on well. Battle after battle was fought, and he conducted himself like a brave soldier as he was. He was promoted again and again. His letters home were all full of hope and encouragement. Sometimes these letters were written in the quiet tent, and sometimes they were rough, pencilled lines, written hurriedly on the back of a knapsack, while resting from a weary march. The time passed swiftly on, and every one was hoping that the sad strife would soon be ended.

Then came the greatest struggle of the war. Thousands fell on both sides, and sorrow took her seat by many firesides all over the land. Ellen Boone received a letter one day that was written in a strange hand. She hastily tore it open, and read as follows :—

'DEAR ELLEN,—These lines are written for me by the ward-master of the hospital. In the last battle, I lost my arms. They have both been taken off close to the shoulder, and now I am a cripple for life. I send this note to tell you that you must not think any more of marrying me. I can never care for you now, as a husband ought to care for as good a wife as you would be. You are released from all the precious promises you have given me. They say I am doing well. Our regiment was badly cut up.

'Affectionately yours,

'JAMES RIVERS.'

No answer was ever written to that letter. James Rivers was alone for a few days in the great hospital, but he was not alone one day longer than it took to make a certain journey. One afternoon there were quick footsteps on the hospital stairs, and a lady was seen walking hastily down the aisle that led to the place where that armless soldier was lying. All the patients in the hospital were astonished, when they saw her kneel down at his bedside, and put her arms tenderly round his neck. And then, like a true and faithful woman as she was, she spoke the best words of all her life, when she said : ' James, don't mind the lost arms too much. You are dearer to me now than when you had them. I will never let you leave me again.'

But Jesus loves us a hundred times more than that noble-hearted woman loved the wounded soldier to whom she was engaged. And the more feeble and helpless and needy we are, the greater is His willingness to save us and bless us. And the second reason why we should seek Him as our Saviour is because He has great willingness to help.

But then Jesus has GREAT TENDERNESS, *as well as great power and willingness ;* and this is the third reason why we should take Him as our Saviour.

Sometimes we meet with good people, who are able to help us, and willing enough too to do it, when we ask them ; but they do it in such a rough way, and they speak so crossly about it, that our feelings are very much hurt, and we can hardly keep from crying, even when they are doing the very things that we asked them to do. And we go away, feeling that we never shall be willing to ask them to do anything for us again. But ah ! how different it is with Jesus ! He is called ' the

Lamb of God,' because He is always so gentle, and kind, and loving in His ways. The prophet Isaiah said of Him, that ' *He would not break a bruised reed,* nor *quench the smoking flax.*' And Jesus said Himself, when showing how tender He would be in helping His people, 'As one whom *his mother comforteth, so* will I comfort you.'

JOY OVER THE SAVED.

A gentleman was once travelling down the Ohio River in a steamboat. He was acquainted with the captain of the boat. As they were talking together one day, the captain pointed to the pilot, who was standing by the wheel.

'That pilot,' said the captain, 'is a remarkably brave, good fellow, Some weeks ago, he asked me to take the helm. I did so, and he jumped overboard to save the life of a boy, whom he saw struggling in the water. He did it at the risk of his own life. But he saved the boy.'

'I went up to the brave man,' said this gentleman, 'to have a little talk with him.'

'Do you ever see the boy whom you saved ? ' I asked.

'O, yes, Sir ; every trip that we make he comes down to see me.'

'And how do you feel towards him when you see him ? '

'More than I can tell,' said he. 'I feel a deeper interest in that boy than even in any of my own seven children at home, for whom I never ran such risk.'

This gives us a beautiful illustration of what Jesus meant, when He said that there is more joy in heaven over one sinner that repenteth than over ninety-and-nine just persons, like the angels, that need no repentance. And so, wonderful as it appears, it is yet true that when we are trying to serve Jesus, and take Him as our Saviour, He feels a more tender interest in us than He does in any of the angels of heaven. And the reason is that He died for us; but He never died for the angels.

HE CARRIES THEM UP THE HILL.

Some children had once been committing to memory the twenty-third Psalm, — that beautiful psalm—in which David speaks of God as his shepherd. After they had learned their lesson, they went on talking about what Jesus, the Good Shepherd, does for His sheep and lambs.

'He guides them,' said one of the children, 'and feeds them, and drives away the bears and lions from them.'

'Yes,' said the smallest child among them; 'and *He carries them up the hills.*' This is true; and it shows us how great the tenderness of Jesus is. I suppose this dear child was thinking of that sweet passage in which the prophet Isaiah, when speaking of Jesus, said: 'He shall feed His flock like a shepherd : He shall *gather the lambs with His arm, and carry them in His bosom.*' (Isaiah xl. 11.)

'I TAKE CARE OF MY LAMBS.'

A gentleman in England was walking over his farm one day with a friend, and was taking great pleasure in showing him his orchards, his crops, his herds of cattle, and flocks of sheep. The visitor was very much pleased with everything that he saw on the farm ; but nothing pleased him so much as the splendid sheep which this gentleman had. He had seen the same breed of sheep before, but these were the largest, and strongest, and finest looking he had ever seen. With great earnestness, he said to his friend, ' Do tell me how you manage to raise such splendid-looking sheep as these.' His answer was :—

' I take care of my lambs, Sir.'

But no shepherd ever took such tender care of his lambs as Jesus does. And when we know how much He loves us, and how tenderly He feels towards us, we need not fear to trust Him for anything that we want.

IF YOU LOVE ME, LEAN HARD.

An American lady was labouring as a missionary in Turkey. Her health was poor, and she was feeling very feeble. One hot Sunday afternoon she sat on her mat in the chapel, hardly able to keep her place, and longing for something to lean on for support till the service was over. Several of the native women who had been converted were sitting by her. Presently she felt one of these women getting up close behind her, and heard her whisper, ' Lean on me.' She did not notice it at first. Then the whisper was repeated, ' Lean on me.' She leaned a little on the kind-hearted woman, who with great earnestness repeated the whispered words, ' If you love me, *lean hard.* How kind and tender and thoughtful this was! Yet this is just the way in which those who truly love us always feel. But nobody loves us as Jesus does. Nobody is so tender and kind as He is. And there is no one on whom we may *lean so hard,* and whom we can trust so confidently for everything, as we can do with Jesus.

OUR HAND IN CHRIST'S.

A little girl lay on her dying bed. She had been suffering from a sad and painful disease. The doctors

F

had tried all they could to cure her, but in vain.   And now they had given her up.   They could do no more for her.   Not long before, this dear child's step had been as light, her face as bright, and her heart as joyous as those of any of her companions.   But now her body was racked with pain, death was laying his cold hand upon her, and she was soon to enter into eternity.

Her loving father sat by her bedside, watching the look of pain on the pale face of his suffering child.

'Nannie, dear,' he said, with quivering lip, and his eyes filled with tears, ' do you feel sad at the thought of dying ? '

' No, dear papa,' she replied, as a sweet smile lighted up her dying face; ' *my hand is all the while in the hand of Jesus, and He will not let it go.*'

How beautiful this was!   And how tender and loving it was in Jesus to come near in this way to the dear child when she was dying, and take all her fear away by making her feel as if He was holding her hand in His, and would not let it go.

And thus we have spoken of the three things in Jesus which make Him such a wonderful Saviour.   He has *great power*, *great willingness*, and *great tenderness*. And it was because the angel Gabriel knew He had these great things that he said to Joseph, His reputed father, before He was born, ' Thou shalt call His name *Jesus*, for He shall save His people from their sins.'

'IN THE DIM LIGHT OF THE FEEBLE LAMP THAT HUNG NEAR, HE
WAS TRYING TO READ A LITTLE IN THE BIBLE.'—*See page* 92.

V.

JESUS THE WAY.

' I am the way.'—JOHN xiv. 6.

THIS word 'way' may mean either one of two things. It may mean the road along which you must go to reach a certain place. If you are in New York, and wish to go to Liverpool, the way to get there would be to go and take your passage in one of the ocean steamers : then you go on board that steamer, and, if God shall favour the voyage, in due time you will find yourself 'at the haven where you would be.' That is the *way* to Liverpool. This is one meaning of the word 'way.'

But then the word '*way*' has another meaning. Sometimes it means the thing that must be done in order to secure any particular end. For instance, you have a lesson to learn. The only *way* to do this is to sit down and study it, and *keep on* studying till you have learned it. Suppose my watch has run down and stopped. The *way* to make it go again is to take the key and wind it up.

And when we think of heaven, Jesus is the way in both these senses. He is, as it were, the road along which we must walk in order to get there. He has done all that is necessary in order that we may enter heaven. God has promised to take us to heaven, on account of what Jesus has done. If we believe this, and trust in Jesus, we shall certainly be saved. There is a grand old hymn used in the service of the Episcopal Church, called the ' Te Deum.' In one of its verses, the worshippers are led to look up to Jesus, and say: ' *When Thou hadst overcome the sharpness of death, Thou didst open the kingdom of heaven to all believers.*'

' *I am the way.*' This is what Jesus says of Him-self. And the most important things in the Bible are the things it tells about Jesus. He is 'the Sun of Righteousness;' and every passage that tells us any-thing about Him may well be called a ray from this sun. 'I am the way.' These words teach us that Jesus is the way to heaven, or the way of salvation.

And so the subject we have now to consider is,— *Jesus the Way to heaven.* And the question we must try to answer is this : What kind of a way to heaven do we find in Jesus ?

There are *four* things that mark this way of which we are to speak.

In the FIRST *place, the way of salvation through Jesus is a* PLAIN *way.*

Sometimes we have to walk in paths that are not plain. If we get into a paved street or a turnpike road, then we are in a plain way. It is easy to find a way like that, and easy to keep it when it is found. But if we are travelling over a sandy desert, or through a rocky country where there is nothing to mark the path, then we are in a way that is not plain. It is hard to find the way, and hard to keep it when it is found. At every step, we are liable to get off the right track.

But it is different with the way of salvation in Jesus. This is a plain way. It is easy to find and easy to keep, if we only ask God to help us in finding and keeping it. When the prophet Isaiah is speaking of the times of Christ, and of the knowledge of salvation that should then be enjoyed, he says : 'And an highway shall be there, and it shall be called, The way of holiness : the wayfaring men, though fools, shall not err therein.' (Isaiah xxxv. 8.)

And when God gave directions about this way to another of the prophets, He said, ' *Make it plain*, that he may run that readeth it.' (Habakkuk ii. 2.)

And if we consider what is necessary for us to know, in order to walk in this way, we shall see at once how plain it is.

An aged minister in England, whose name was John Newton, once said : ' When I was young, I was sure of many things ; but there are only two things of which I am sure now : one is, that I am a great sinner ; and the other is, that Jesus is a great Saviour.' These are the two most important things in the world for us to know. If we learn to know these two things, we shall know what this way of salvation is, and we shall understand how plain a way it is.

IT IS DARK.

Here is an incident that illustrates how plain and simple the way of salvation in Jesus is.

The father of a little girl was once in great trouble and distress of mind on account of his sins. He lay awake, after going to bed one night, in fear and dread; he felt like a ship tossed about by a storm, and unable to find any rest or peace. The hours of the night were going slowly and wearily by. He could not sleep because of his trouble. His little daughter was sleeping in her crib beside his bed. Presently she

began to move about uneasily. Then he heard her
voice, speaking timidly amidst the darkness :—

'Papa! papa!' she called.

'What is it, my darling?' he asked.

'O, papa, it's so dark. Take Nellie's hand.' He
reached out, and took her tiny little hand, clasping it
firmly in his own. A sigh of relief came from her little
heart. At once she was quieted and comforted. All
her loneliness and fear were gone. She felt that a
loving father was near her, and in a few moments she
was sound asleep again.

That father felt that his little child had taught him
a valuable lesson.

' O, *my* Father in heaven, my Saviour and my God,'
he cried, 'it is dark, very dark in my soul. Take my
hand.'

So he turned to Jesus, and trusted in Him ; and he
had a sweet feeling of peace come over him. ' This is
all I need,' he said. ' Jesus my Saviour *keep hold* of my
hand.'

And this is the way to find peace and salvation.
When we feel afraid on account of our sins or of any
trouble, we must put our hand in the hand of Jesus,
and trust in Him, just as this dear child trusted in her
loving father. This is the way of salvation that Jesus
came to teach us. And this is a simple, plain way.

MAKE IT SO PLAIN THAT I CAN GET HOLD OF IT.

A minister of the gospel had a son who was a
colonel in the army. Tidings came to this father one
day that his son had been wounded in battle, and was
not expected to live. He hastened to the hospital to see
him. On arriving there, he asked the doctor if his son
was in danger. ' He cannot live more than three or

four days,' said the doctor; 'and he may die any moment.'

With a sad heart, the father went in to see his boy; for, though a minister's son, he was not a Christian.

' O, father,' said the wounded man, ' the doctor says I must die, and I am not prepared for it. Tell me how I can be ready. Make it so plain that I can get hold of it.'

'My son,' said the father, ' do you remember one day, years ago, when you came home from school, I had occasion to rebuke you for something you had done? You became very angry, and abused me with harsh language.'

' Yes, father. I was thinking it all over before you came, and I wanted so badly to see you, and ask you once more to forgive me.'

' Do you remember, after your anger had passed off, how you came in and threw your arms round my neck, and said, ' My dear father, I am so sorry for speaking to you in such a wrong way. Won't you forgive me?'

' Yes, I remember it very distinctly.'

' Do you remember what I said to you, as you wept upon my neck? '

' O, yes. You said, "I forgive you with all my heart;" and you kissed me. I shall never forget those words.'

' Did you believe me? '

' Certainly. I never doubted anything you said.'

' And then did you feel happy again.'

' Yes, perfectly happy. And since that time I have always loved you better than ever before. I never shall forget how it relieved me, when you looked so kindly on me, and said, " I forgive you with all my heart." '

' Well, now, my son, this is the way to come to Jesus. Tell Him, "*I am so sorry*," just as you told me;

and He will forgive you a thousand times quicker than I did.'

'Father, is this the way to become a Christian?'

'I don't know any other way, my dear son.'

'Why, father, I can get hold of this. O, I am so glad you came to tell me, and make it all so plain!'

The wounded man turned his head upon his pillow, and lifted up his heart in prayer to Jesus. The poor, distressed father sank into the chair, covered his face with his hands, and wept as only a loving father would do. He wept a long time. Then he felt his boy's trembling hand laid gently on his head, and the word 'father' spoken in such a tone of tenderness and joy, that he felt sure a change had come over him.

'Father, my dear father, I don't want you to weep any more. And you need not. It's all right with me. I am perfectly happy now. Jesus has forgiven me,—I know He has, for He says so ; and I take His word for it, just as I took yours.'

After a while, the doctor came in. He felt the pulse of the wounded man, and said with surprise, 'Why, Colonel, you *look* better.'

'I *am* better, Doctor. I'm going to get well.'

He did get well; and he is living now, the joy and comfort of that father who made the way of salvation so plain that he could get hold of it.

'Jesus said, 'I am the way.' The way of salvation in Jesus is a *plain* way.

The SECOND *thing about this way for us to consider is that it is* A BROAD *way.*

I mean by this that it is wide enough to take in all sorts of people. Jesus was showing how broad the way of salvation is when He said : ' Come unto Me, *all* ye that labour and are heavy laden, and I will give you rest.' (Matthew xi. 28.) And the Apostle John was showing the same thing when he said : ' *Whosoever* will, let him come and take the water of life freely.' (Revelation xxii. 17.) Jesus was showing the same thing about this way when He said : ' *Whatsoever* ye shall ask of the Father in My name, He may give it you.' (John xv. 16.)

These words, ' *whosoever* ' and ' *whatsoever*,' are two of the most precious words connected with the way of salvation. ' Whosoever ' is on the outside of the gate that opens into this way, and it tells us that any one may come in who wants to. ' *Whatsoever* ' is on the inside the gate, and shows us that those who enter this way, and walk in it, can get everything they need to make them safe and happy.

Here are some sweet and simple lines, written about a conversation among some children in reference to this word :—

' WHOSOEVER.'

There were children on the floor,
Conning Bible verses o'er.

' Which word, all the Bible through,
Do you love the best ?' asked Sue.

' I like " faith " the best,' said one.
' " Jesus " is my word alone.'

' I like " hope," ' and I like " love ;" '
' I like " heaven," our home above.'

One, more small than all the rest,
' I like " whosoever " best.

' " Whosoever," that means all,—
Even I, who am so small.

" Whosoever !" Ah ! I see ;
That 's the word for you and me.

' Whosoever will ' may come ;
Find a pardon and a home.

Here is an incident which shows how true these lines are about this word ' whosoever ':

A SAILOR SAVED.

There was a poor sailor who had lived a very wicked life, as sailors are very apt to do. Once, while far off at sea on a long voyage, it pleased God to awaken his conscience and show him what a sinner he was. Then he was in great distress. The thought that he might die in his sins and be lost for ever was terrible to him. There was no one on board the ship to give him any help, or tell him what to do. But he read his Bible whenever he had a chance. One night he lay in his berth in the forecastle. His shipmates were all asleep around him. In the dim light of the feeble lamp that hung near, he was trying to read a little in the Bible. He came to the sixteenth verse of the third chapter of John : ' God so loved the world, that He gave His only begotten Son, that whosoever believeth in Him should not perish, but have everlasting life.' He put his finger on this word ' whosoever,' and thought about it. ' Whosoever,' said he ; ' that means anybody : that means everybody. Why, that means *me* ! '

Then he turned in faith to Jesus, and He received him. He got into the broad way of salvation through this sweet word ' whosoever.'

THE LOST RESTORED.

One day, a minister in one of our large cities was visiting with a friend among some of the poorest of the population. He stopped in front of a wretched-looking house, and knocked at the door. No one answered. He opened the door and went in. A rickety bedstead, a couple of broken chairs, the remains of a table, and a few pieces of earthenware on the shelf, made up all the furniture of the room. It was the very picture of wretchedness and want. In the middle of the room, a miserable-looking woman lay on the floor drunk. That was her home. She was a widow. She had three children, who were not then at home.

The minister said to his friend, 'Here is a wretched, ruined woman going to the judgment-seat with all her sins upon her head. Let us pray for her.' They kneeled down, and the minister offered an earnest prayer that God would have mercy on this poor woman, that He would turn her from her sins, and save her soul for Jesus' sake.

She lay there still and stupid, and seemed to take no notice of what was done or said.

The minister and his friend went away. Some months after, that minister was going again through that part of the city. A well-dressed, respectable-looking woman came up and spoke to him.

'I think you must be mistaken, Madam,' said the minister.

'No, Sir, I am not. Do you not remember going into a house in this neighbourhood some months since, and praying over a woman who lay drunk on the floor?'

'I do.'

'Well, Sir, I am that woman. I was respectably brought up by Christian parents. I married; but after a while my husband died, and left me with three children in utter poverty. I saw no way of support for myself and children but by my own shame. Then I took to drinking to drown my sorrow. I was at the lowest point of sin and misery when you stopped and offered that prayer over me. I thank you for it. That prayer saved me. It carried me back to my early days. It

made me think of my dear mother, now in heaven.
And, by God's help, I hope yet to join her there.'

O, it *is* a broad way of salvation that can take in
such poor, wretched creatures as this!

BECAUSE I AXED HIM.

A gentleman who teaches a class of boys on Sunday
evening was sent for once to visit one of his class, a
news-boy, named Billy, who was very ill.

As he entered the room, Billy said, 'O, Captain,
I 'm mighty glad to see yer.'

'What can I do for you, my dear fellow? Shall I
get you a nurse, or some medicine, or something nice
to eat?' asked the teacher.

'No, Captain, it wasn't that I wanted yer for. I
wanted to ax yer two questions. The first is this:
Did you tell us the other night as how Jesus Christ
died for every feller?'

'Yes, I did; for the Bible says that Jesus Christ
tasted death for every man.'

'Good!' said Billy; 'I thought so. Now I 've
another question. Did you tell us as how Jesus Christ
saves every feller that axes Him?'

'Yes,' said his friend; 'for the Bible says, "Every
one that asketh receiveth."'

'Then I know,' said Billy, with a feeble but happy
voice, 'that He saves me, because I axes Him.'

The teacher paused to wipe away a tear from his
eye. Then he stooped down to speak to the boy. But
Billy's head had dropped back on his pillow of rags,
and his happy spirit had gone to Jesus.

Jesus says, 'I am the way.' The way of salvation
that we find in Jesus is a plain way, and a broad way.

In the THIRD *place, we may speak of the way to heaven which we have in Jesus as* A NARROW *way.*

And here perhaps some of you may think that I am contradicting myself; because, after trying to prove that this way is broad, I am now declaring that it is narrow too. But there is no contradiction here. We have seen how truly it is a broad way, and that it is a narrow way also is just as true. But it is not broad and narrow both in the same sense. It is a broad way in one sense, and a narrow in another and very different sense. It is a broad way, as we have seen, because the greatest sinners may come into it, and any number of them may come. It is a narrow way, because when sinners come into it *they must leave all their sins behind.* It is so broad that the greatest sinner who ever lived may come into it; but at the same time it is so narrow that not the least sin can be allowed to enter it. And this is what Jesus meant when He said, 'Broad is the way that leadeth to destruction, and many there be who go in thereat; but narrow is the way that leadeth unto life, and few there be that find it.' (Matthew vii. 13.)

If we wish to walk in this way, we must give up everything that we know to be sinful.

For example, there is a vessel lying at anchor. That anchor, you know, goes down to the bottom of the water. There it sinks in the mud, or clings to the rock, and holds the vessel fast. It can make no progress while the anchor holds it. It may rise and fall, as the tide rises or falls; but it cannot move away from the place it occupies. The sailors may unfurl the sails, and the wind may fill them. And now, if the anchor were only taken up, how quickly that vessel would begin to move, and how rapidly it would go on its way! But the anchor prevents all this. It keeps it in one place all the time. And just what the anchor does to

the vessel, one sin, one wrong thought or feeling in-
dulged or allowed, will do for the soul. It will keep it
from going on in the way of salvation. Jesus will not
save us, unless we are willing to give up every sin, and
let go every other dependence, and trust to Him alone.

LET GO THAT BRANCH.

A lady once was led to see that she was a sinner.
The thought of her sins made her feel very unhappy.
She mourned and wept over them day after day. She
went to see her minister. He talked and prayed with
her; but she could find no peace nor comfort. The
difficulty was just here. She had been a very charitable
woman, and had given away a great deal of money to
the poor. She wanted to trust in part to these good
works. These, she knew, would not be enough of themselves to save her; but yet she thought they ought to
be reckoned for something. They would not pay the
whole price of her salvation, but still it seemed to her
they ought to go for part of the price. She was not
willing to give up her trust in these good works,—not
willing to let everything else go, and trust to Jesus
alone as her Saviour.

One night, after weeping and praying in great
distress, she went to bed and fell asleep. In her sleep
she had a dream. She thought, in her dream, that,
while standing on the brink of a dreadful precipice, she
fell over. In falling, she caught hold of the branch of
a tree, and clung desperately to it. In her terror, while
still clinging to the tree, she cried out, ' O, save me,
save me!' She heard the voice of some one standing
below, and calling to her. She recognised it in her
dream as the voice of Jesus her Saviour. The voice
rang out in clear, distinct tones, saying, ' Let go that
branch, and I will save you.'

But she was unwilling to loose her hold on the tree. Again she cried,—

'O, save me, save me!'

The same voice was heard again, saying: 'I cannot help you while you cling there. Let go that branch, and I will save you.'

At last she made up her mind to do this. She let go the branch, expecting to be dashed to pieces on the rocks below. But, instead of this, she found herself caught in the strong, encircling arms of her loving Saviour. In the joy of feeling herself safe, she awoke. And so in her dream she had learned the lesson which she had failed to learn in her waking hours. She saw that the way of salvation was too narrow for her to carry any of her good works into it. She made up her mind not to depend on her charities or good works any more. She saw that these were the branch she was clinging to, so that Jesus could not save her. She resolved to let go this branch, to give these all up, and trust only to Jesus. She turned to Him, saying, in the language of the hymn,—

'Nothing in my hand I bring,
Simply to Thy Cross I cling ;
Naked, come to thee for dress ;
Helpless, look to thee for grace ;
Guilty, to the fountain fly :
Wash me, Saviour, or I die.'

And so we see how it is that the way of salvation in Jesus is a *narrow* way.

There is one other thing about this way to speak of ; and that is,—It is the ONLY *way.*

Some people think that there are a great many ways to heaven, and that one of these is as good as any of the

G

others. Now what I think or say on this subject, or
what any other man thinks or says about it, is of very
little consequence. The important question to ask here
is, What does *God* say about it? There are two passages in the Bible in which God speaks out very plainly
on this point. In one, He says distinctly, ' *Besides Me
there is no Saviour.*' (Isaiah xliii. 11.) In the other,
speaking through the Apostle Peter about Jesus, God
says, ' *Neither is there salvation in any other : for there is
none other name under heaven given among men, whereby
we must be saved.*' (Acts iv. 12.) No one can ever get
to heaven who does not go there through Jesus Christ.
Many will go to heaven without knowing how they get
there. But they will find it was Jesus alone who
brought them there. When infants and young children
die, they all go to heaven. But they do not go there
because they have never committed any actual sin. It
is true they have not sinned themselves ; but they have
a sinful nature. Their hearts are sinful. They could
not be happy there unless their hearts were changed.
But Jesus does this for them, and then takes them to
heaven because He died for them. If we are hoping to
get to heaven in any other way than through the merits
and death of Jesus, we shall find ourselves mistaken.
Jesus is the *only* way.

JESUS WILL GO WITH ME.

A little girl only four years old was taken sick, and
was very ill. One day her father was sitting by her
bedside. She turned to him, and asked this question :
' Papa, does the doctor think I shall die ? '
With a very sad heart, her father said,—
' My darling, the doctor is afraid you cannot live.'
Then her pale face grew very sad. She thought awhile
about the dark graves, into which she had sometimes

looked down, where people were buried. Her eyes
filled with tears, as she said,—

'Papa, the grave is dark. O, it's *very* dark. Won't
you go down with me into it ? '

With a bursting heart, her father told her he could
not go with her, till the Lord called him.

'Papa, won't you let mamma go with me ? '

It almost broke that father's heart to tell his darling
child that, much as her mother loved her, she could not
go with her either.

The poor dear child turned her face to the wall and
wept. Young as she was, she had been taught about
Jesus, as the Friend and Saviour of sinners. She
poured out her little heart to Him with a child's full
faith, and found comfort in Him. Soon she turned
again to her father, with her face all lighted up with
joy, and said,—

'Papa, the grave is not dark now. Jesus will go
with me.'

But there was no one else in all the world who
could have done this for that dying child. And when
you and I come to stand as near to the grave as this
dear child was, we shall want, as she did, some one to
go with us into the dark and lonely grave. But Jesus
is the *only* one who can do this. And when this dear
child said, 'The grave is not dark now, for Jesus will
go with me,' she was feeling the same comfort that
David, the famous king of Israel, felt, three thousand
years ago, when he said, 'Yea, though I walk through
the valley of the shadow of death, I will fear no evil;
for *Thou art with me.*' (Psalm xxiii. 4.)

WHICH WAY SHALL I TAKE ?

Some years ago, there was a distinguished lawyer in

this country, who had an only child, a daughter about sixteen years old. She was the light and joy of her father's life. His heart seemed to be bound up in her.

The mother of this young girl was an earnest Christian woman. She had tried to teach her child that Jesus was the only way of salvation, and to make her a Christian. But her husband was an infidel. He had told his daughter not to believe the Bible, and that we could get to heaven without the help of Jesus. This daughter loved and honoured both her parents, and they were both worthy of her love and honour. But as her father told her of one way to heaven, and her mother told her of another way, she could not make up her mind which of these two ways was the right one. Under these circumstances, it is not surprising that she grew up to the age of sixteen without becoming a Christian. But then she was taken very ill. It soon became plain that she was going to die. She thought about her soul and heaven, but could not make up her mind whether her mother's way or her father's way was the right way to take.

One day, when her father was in the room, she said to him with great earnestness : 'Father, I am going to die. I want my soul to be saved. What must I do to be saved? My mother has taught me that the *only* way of salvation is in Jesus Christ. You have taught me that we can be saved without Jesus. Here are two entirely different ways. They cannot both be right. *Which* is the right one? The time has come when I must choose one or the other of these ways. What shall I do? Father, shall I take my mother's way, or shall I take yours ? '

That strong man was deeply moved. He covered his face with his hands, and walked up and down the room in the deepest distress. After a while, he came to the bedside of his daughter. He took her pale, thin hand in his, kissed it fondly, and bathed it with tears, as he said slowly, but solemnly,—

'My darling daughter, take your mother's way.'

Here is a ship at sea. She has been overtaken by a dreadful storm. She has struggled long with that storm, but she can do so no longer. Her masts are broken, her sails are rent. She has sprung a leak. The crew have worked at the pumps day and night; but now the pumps are choked, and can no longer be worked. The water is rising in the hold of the ship. It is very evident that she cannot be kept afloat much longer. Sooner or later she must sink in the mighty waters. There is only one way left to the poor sailors for saving their lives. What is that? It is to *take to the life-boat.* If they can launch the lifeboat, and manage to get into it, they may be saved. It is impossible for them to expect safety in any other way. *That* is the *only* way of safety for them.

And we, as sinners, are just in the position of such a storm-tossed wreck at sea. We are in danger of being lost at any time. We are sure of perishing at last, unless some way of escape is found. Jesus is *the only* way. *He is the life-boat.* There is no other way of escape for us: Let us take to this life-boat. Let us turn to Jesus, and trust in Him. Jesus says, 'I am the way.'

This way of salvation is a PLAIN way—a BROAD way—a NARROW way—the ONLY way.

As we think of the words of this text, let us look to Jesus, and offer the prayer of the hymn, which says,—

'Thou art the Way, the Truth, the Life;
Grant us that Way to know,
That Truth to keep, that Life to win,
Whose joys eternal flow.'

'AFTER A WHILE, SHE WAS SEEN WALKING IN THE GARDEN, TALKING TO HER POOR, SOILED DOLLY.'—*See page* 110.

VI.

JESUS THE TRUTH.

' I am the truth.'—JOHN xiv. 6.

HOW many do two and two make? Four. And what do we call that branch of study which teaches us about numbers, how to add them up, and subtract and divide them? We call it Arithmetic. And it is a truth in arithmetic that two and two make four. Now suppose that we have a blackboard here. Suppose we draw a house on one side of it, and another house on the other side. And then suppose we draw several lines from one of these houses to the other. One of these lines is full of curves, another is a zigzag line, and another is a straight line. Which of these three lines will give us the shortest distance from one of those houses to the other? The straight line. That study which teaches us all about lines and curves and angles we call Geometry. And it is a truth in geometry that ' the shortest distance between any two points is a straight line.' When we are learning geography, we are told that an island is what? A portion of land entirely surrounded by water. And what is a peninsula? A portion of land almost surrounded by water. These are truths in what? In geography. Who discovered America? Christopher Columbus. Who was the first president of the United States? George

Washington. And what do we call the study which teaches us all about different nations? We call it History. And the facts just referred to are truths of history. And the study which teaches us about God, and how to love and serve Him, we call Religion. And the truths that we are taught about God or heaven we speak of as truths in religion. But Jesus has so much to do with our religion, and what the Bible teaches us about it, that we sometimes put His sweet and precious name in place of the word religion, or in place of the Bible; and then, instead of saying of a certain doctrine that it is a truth of the Bible or a truth in religion, we may say that it is *a truth in Jesus.*

And so, we see, there are a great many kinds of truth. There are truths in arithmetic, and truths in geometry, and truths in history, and truths in geography, and truths in religion; or, as we have just said, these latter truths may be called '*truth as it is in Jesus.*' And this is what Jesus means when He says, '*I am* THE TRUTH.' What this teaches us is that truth in Jesus is the best of all truth. It is better for us to know what the Bible teaches about Him than to know everything else in the world besides. This is our subject to-day. *The truth in Jesus is the best of all truth.* And the reasons for this we shall see, as soon as we begin to consider what this truth does for us.

I wish to show that there are *three* things which the truth in Jesus does for us. These are things that no other truth in the world can do; and thus we know that this is the best truth. It may help us to remember these three things, if we bear in mind that each of them begins with the letter *S.*

Jesus says, '*I am the truth.*' *Now, in the* FIRST

place, the truth in Jesus is the best of all truth, because it SANCTIFIES, OR MAKES US GOOD.

To sanctify, means to make good or holy. And the pattern, or model of goodness, set before us in the Bible is the example of Jesus. He is the best, the most perfect of all beings. In the language of the hymn we sometimes sing, we may well ask,—

' O, who 's like Jesus ? '

And if it were possible for us to go with this question to the angels of heaven, as well as the inhabitants of all the other worlds that God has made, we should come back to our own world without finding a better answer to the question we had taken with us than the words of the same hymn, which tell us,—

' There 's *none* like Jesus.'

There is none like Him in heaven; none like Him in the earth; and none like Him in any other world. He is ' *the chief among ten thousand, and altogether lovely.*'

And that which helps to make us like Jesus is the very best thing in the world for us. Now to be a true Christian is to be like Jesus. It is to tread ' in the blessed steps of His most holy life.' It is to ' learn of Him to be meek and lowly in heart.' It is the truth the Bible teaches us about Jesus, which makes us Christians in the beginning. And then it is only by knowing more of this truth that we ' grow in grace,' or become better Christians.

Now let us look at some examples of those who have learned to know the ' truth as it is in Jesus,' and we shall see that this is the truth which sanctifies us, or makes us good.

Let us take our first example from the New Testa-

ment. It is that of the first martyr Stephen. The
Jews were angry with him, on account of his preaching. A great crowd gathered round him, to put him
to death by stoning. In the presence of those angry
men, who were thirsting for his blood, he kneeled down,
and offered this prayer : ' Lord, lay not this sin to their
charge !' How truly had he learned to be like Jesus !
You remember how He prayed for His murderers, who
had just nailed Him to the cross, saying, ' *Father, forgive
them, for they know not what they do.*'

It was the power of the truth in Jesus that made
Stephen so much like His blessed Master. And that
truth has the same power now that it had then.

THE SPIRIT OF THE MARTYR STEPHEN.

There was an account in the papers, the other day,
of a man who showed that he had just the same spirit.
His name was Joseph Robbins. He was a bridge watchman on one of our railways. He was murdered by a
neighbour, who wanted to rob him of his money. The
murderer was caught directly after. During the trial,
he made this confession in open court :—

' I knew that Robbins had just received his month's
wages, and I resolved to have his money. I got a
shot gun, and went to the bridge. As I came near the
watch-house, on looking through the window, I saw
Robbins sitting inside. His head and shoulders only
could be seen. I raised the gun, took aim, and fired.
I waited a few minutes, to see if the report of the gun
had alarmed any one. But all was still. Then I went
up to the watch-house door, and found Robbins on his
knees praying. I listened, and heard him say, " O God,
have mercy on the man who did this, and spare him for
Jesus' sake." I was horrified. I did not dare to enter
the house. I couldn't touch that man's money. Instead

of this, I turned and ran away, I knew not whither. His words have haunted me ever since.'

Now the prayer of this humble man was more re- markable even than the prayer of Saint Stephen. The death of Stephen was not so sudden as that of the watch- man. He knew what the Jews were going to do with him, and he had time to think about his prayer before he offered it. But Robbins was altogether unprepared for what took place. He had no expectation of being killed. But no sooner did the shot strike him than he fell on his knees and prayed, not for himself, but for his murderer, without even knowing who he was. This man had the very spirit of Jesus. And it was knowing and believing the truth in Jesus which put this spirit in him. It was this truth which had sanctified him, or made him so good. And the truth that can do this for us is the best of all truth.

THE SHORT MEASURE.

When we have been reading the Bible, or learning a Sunday-school lesson, or hearing a sermon, we ought to try and practise what we have been taught. A poor woman, who kept a retail shop, was asked once, after going to church, what she remembered about the sermon. She said: 'I can't recall the text, nor tell just what the minister said; but I know he preached about short weights and measures; and all that I can say is this, that I went home and *burnt my short bushel.*' That was the best use she could possibly have made of the sermon.

Here is another story to show how it is that the truth we hear about Jesus does us good and helps to make us better. This story is told of a good, honest

Irishwoman, whose name was Molly Malone. She used to say, after hearing a good sermon, ' Sure, and it's mighty improvin'.' But she could never give any other account of the sermon than this : ' It's mighty improvin'.'

Molly was a washerwoman. One day the minister found her hanging out her clothes on the hedge to dry, and he made up his mind to try to find out what she meant by the remark she always made about the sermon. So he began : ' Well, Molly, how did you like the sermon you heard yesterday ? '

' Plase yer riverence, and it was mighty improvin'.'

' And what part of it did you like best ? '

' Well, sure, and I liked every part of it.'

' But I suppose there were some parts of it you were more struck with than you were with others.'

' In troth, plase yer riverence, I don't remember any part exactly ; but sure and it was mighty improvin'.'

' Now, Molly, how could it be improving, if you don't remember any part of it ? '

' Well, now, yer riverence sees that linen I 've been washing and dhrying on the hedge there ? '

' O, certainly.'

' Wasn't it the soap and the wather that made the linen clane ? '

' Of course they did.'

' And isn't the linen all the better for it ? '

' O, no doubt of that, Molly.'

' But not a dhrop of the soap and wather stays in it. Well, Sir, it's the same thing wid me. Not a word of the sarmint stays in me. I suppose it all dhries out of me ; but I'm the better and the claner for it when it's over, for all that.'

A CHILD'S WISH.

A group of little children were talking together. Presently this question was started: ' What is the thing you wish for most ? ' Some said one thing, and some said another. At last it came to the turn of a little boy, ten years old, to speak. This was his answer : ' *I wish to live without sinning.*'

What an excellent answer this was ! King Solomon in all his glory, and with all his wisdom, could not have given a better. But it was knowing and believing the truth in Jesus that put this wish into that dear boy's heart.

THE THISTLE IN THE HEART.

' I 've come again, mamma,' said little Lillie White, quietly peeping into the chamber where her mother was writing. ' Lillie couldn't help it, mamma.'

' And what 's the matter with my little girl this time ? ' said her mother, laying down her pen. ' You haven't got another thistle in your finger, have you ? '

' No, mamma ; the finger is well now ; but there is something stinging me here in my bosom. You needn't unfasten my dress, mamma. You couldn't see it,—it 's deep. I know what it is : it 's wrong feeling there. I hate Carrie Marsh, mamma. She is never good to any of us. But her aunt in New York sends her the prettiest things you ever saw. Now she has sent her a blue dress, and a doll all dressed in pink and white. She brought 'em to me to look at, and said, " You can't have such pretty things, Lillie White." That made me hate her. I know it is wrong to have this feeling, and it stings in my heart worse than the thistle did in my finger. Won't you take *this* out too, mamma ? '

' Only Jesus can take out a sting like this,' said her mother, putting her arms very gently round her darling's neck. ' Go to your room, my dear child, and kneel down and tell Jesus all about your trouble. Ask Him to forgive you for giving way to wrong feeling, and to take away the sting from your heart.'

The little girl slipped away from her mother's arms, and went to her own room. After a while, she was seen walking in the garden, talking to her poor, soiled dolly, and kissing its face as lovingly as Carrie Marsh could have done with her fine, new one. By-and-by she raised her bright and smiling face to the window, and, seeing her mother looking down, she said,—

' It 's all right now, mamma. Jesus has taken away the thistle from my heart just as you took away the one from my finger.'

And it was the truth she had learned about Jesus which led this dear child to do as she did when this thistle was in her heart. And this is the best of all truth, because it will lead us to try and get all the thistles out of our hearts. And this illustrates very well the point now before us. It shows us that the truth in Jesus is the best of all truth, because it sanctifies or makes us good.

Jesus says, '*I am the truth.*' *This is the best of all truths, because in the* SECOND *place it* SATISFIES AND MAKES US HAPPY.

You know how it is with the body when it is hungry. That is a very disagreeable feeling. And when we have it, nothing will take it away, and make us feel comfortable, but to have good bread or some other substantial food to eat. God gave that bread or that food on purpose to take away the terrible feeling we have when hungry, by satisfying our hunger and making us feel comfortable.

And it is just so with the soul. It may be hungry as well as the body. And the hunger of the soul is more painful, and harder to bear than the hunger of the body. Suppose you go to a person whose soul is in trouble on account of some great sorrow or sin, and try to comfort him by telling him one of the truths in arithmetic or geography of which we have spoken. You say to him: ' Never mind, my friend. Don't be troubled: because two and two make four; or because the sun rises in the east and sets in the west; or because George Washington was the first president of the United States.' Do you think that would satisfy him, or do him any good? None whatever. But suppose that instead of this, you go to that person in distress, and tell him ' the old, old story of Jesus and His love.' And suppose he believes what you tell him about ' the truth as it is in Jesus;' will this do him any good, and make him comfortable? Yes, it certainly will. It is the food that this hungry soul needs and craves. This will satisfy it, and make it happy.

Let us look at some examples of the way in which the truth in Jesus does this for those who believe it.

A SERMON IN STONE.

The Princess Elizabeth, daughter of King Charles I. of England, lies buried in Newport Church, in the Isle of Wight. A marble monument erected by Queen Victoria shows, in a very touching way, what her feelings were about the matter of which we are now speaking, at the time of her death. During the time of her

father's troubles, she was a prisoner in Carisbrook
Castle, in that same beautiful island. While there, she
had a long spell of sickness. She was alone, separated
from all the friends and companions of her youth, and
lingered on in her sorrows, till death came and set her
free. She was found one day dead in her bed, with her
Bible open before her, and her finger resting on these
words : ' *Come unto Me, all ye that labour, and are heavy
laden, and I will give you rest.*'

And this is what the monument in Newport is intended to show. It consists of a female figure repre-
senting the young princess. Her head is bowed in
death ; while her hand rests on a marble book before
her, with her finger pointing to the words just quoted,
which are engraved on that book. How touching
this is ! What a sermon in stone that monument
preaches ! To every one who looks at it, it seems to
say : ' Riches and rank cannot make you happy. Jesus
only can satisfy the soul. If you would be truly happy
in life and in death, in this world and the world to
come, seek to know and believe the truth as it is in
Jesus ! '

Here is another sweet illustration of this same
blessed truth. We may call it

THE HAPPY SKIPPER.

This word ' skipper ' is what sailors generally use
for the captain of their vessel.

Not long ago, there lived a good Christian fisher-
man in the village of St. Monance, on the coast of Fife,
in Scotland. His name was Andrew Davidson, and he
was the owner and captain of a fishing-boat called *The
Rose in June*. The herring season came, and Andrew

Davidson and his little crew prepared to go to sea. He had but lately been married, and before leaving home he knelt down with his young wife and asked God to keep her safely while he was away; but she noticed, and her heart sank within her at the thought, that he said not a word about his own safety.

The night after *The Rose in June* sailed with a fleet of other vessels, a terrible storm raged all along the coast. Early the next morning, a crowd of women and children, made up of the families of the absent fishermen, gathered on the beach. Every eye was strained across the waters, to catch the first glimpse of the returning boats. One by one they struggled in ; and shouts of joy and thankfulness arose from one and another, as a husband, a brother, a father, or a son sprang ashore. But *The Rose in June* did not come. Driven by the storm and dashed upon the rocks, she had become a total wreck. Turned bottom upwards, her crew of six men clung to her sides with desperate energy. No other boat was near to help or save them and all around the wild waves were rolling and roaring, threatening every moment to tear each man from his hold, and dash him to pieces on the sharp rocks. Andrew Davidson thought of Jesus in that hour of peril ; and, in the face of certain death, that thought did for him what nothing else in the world could have done,—it made him happy. It may have been that he remembered then how Paul and Silas glorified God in the prison of Philippi ; for he shouted, loud and clear above the storm, ' Now, boys, let 's sing a hymn of praise to God ! ' and at once he began and sang this verse :—

> ' My God, I am Thine,
> What a comfort divine,
> What a blessing to know
> That my Jesus is mine !'

H

These were his last words. He had hardly finished the verse, when a huge wave dashed over him with great force, and in an instant he was swept far away

'From every stormy wind that blows'

into the haven of eternal rest.

A sad silence fell upon the men who had been trying to join in that song of praise. For a while no one spoke. At last, John Allan, the mate of the little vessel, who was also a believer in Jesus, exclaimed,—

'Come, my lads, let us go on with the hymn that our skipper is now finishing in heaven.' And then those brave men, rocking on their wrecked boat, with the waves dashing and the wild winds wailing around them, sang on till they had finished the hymn. The last verse reads thus :—

'And this I shall prove,
Till with joy I remove
To the heaven of heavens
In Jesus's love.'

Just as they were finishing these last words, another huge wave burst over the boat, and the young mate was carried away to join his friend and shipmate in that blessed world,

'Where, anchored safe, his weary soul
Shall find eternal rest,
And not a wave of trouble roll
Across his peaceful breast.'

The rest of the crew of that wrecked boat escaped with their lives. But they never forgot the scene they had witnessed during that terrible storm. And no sermon ever preached about the preciousness of Jesus could make such an impression on their minds as was made by that memorable scene. They felt, deep down into their very souls, that the truth in Jesus is the best of all truth, because it satisfies us and makes us happy.

'*I am the truth.*' And the THIRD *reason why the truth in Jesus is the best of all truth is because it* SAVES US.

But this is what no other kind of knowledge will or can do. You may understand all about the different kinds of knowledge that are taught in our schools and colleges. You may know all about arithmetic, and algebra, and mathematics, and geography, and history, and botany, and astronomy, and this knowledge may be very useful to you in the business of this life, but it will not be of the least use to you in trying to get to heaven. If some poor soul, distressed about his sins, should come to you and ask the question, 'What must I do to be saved?' you would find nothing in all those studies that would be the least help to you in answering that question.

But if you only know what the Bible teaches about Jesus, you will be able to answer this question in a moment. It is the truth in Jesus alone which shows us the way to heaven. If we know and believe this, we are sure to be saved. And when Jesus says, 'I am the truth,' what He means by it is this : that the knowledge of Himself—that is, of what His character is, and what the work is that He has done for us—is the most important of all knowledge. This is the truth that anctifies or makes us good. This is the truth that satisfies us and makes us happy. And this is the truth that saves us.

Now let us look at some illustrations of the way in which 'the truth as it is in Jesus' saves us. And remember that all the truth about God that we find in the Bible is truth in Jesus. It is all saving truth.

THE PICKPOCKET'S STORY.

Some years since, a respectable-looking person introduced himself to two Christian men in London who were a committee of the Bible Society, and were making collections for that society. He said to them:—

'Gentlemen, here are five guineas for your excellent society. I thank God for the good work you are doing. Listen for a moment to my story, and you will see that I have reason enough to thank God for the Bible.

'Not long ago, I belonged to a company of pickpockets. About a year since, two of my companions and myself were passing by a church that was full of people. It was the anniversary of the Bible Society. Seeing so many there, we thought it would be a good chance for us to get some money, by carrying on our wicked business. The church was so crowded that we were obliged to separate from each other. I got into the middle aisle, just in front of the speakers. The Ten Commandments, in large gilt letters, were on the wall behind the pulpit. The first words that caught my eye were: "*Thou shalt not steal.*" In a moment, my attention was arrested. I felt as if God were speaking to me. My conscience troubled me, and my tears began to flow. My companions made signs to me to begin our work; but I took no notice of them. As soon as the meeting was over, I hurried away to a distant part of the city where no one knew me. I got a Bible, and for the first time in my life I began to read it. It showed me what a great sinner I was; but it showed me also what a great Saviour Jesus is. I prayed to Jesus with all my heart. He heard my prayer. And now my sins are pardoned, and my soul is saved in Him. I am on the point of starting for America. But, before going, I want to make a little offering to the

Bible cause. Please accept these five guineas, and may God bless you in the good work you are doing.'

THE SAVING WORD.

When the public drinking fountains were opened in London, it was determined, by the society that opened them, that every fountain should have some text of Scripture engraved upon it. The passage selected for one of them contained these words of Solomon : ' The fear of the Lord is a fountain of life.' (Proverbs xiv. 27.)

One evening two young men passed by this fountain. The elder of them was a barman in a public-house ; the younger one was his brother, who had just come in from the country, to try to find employment in busy London. The barman was telling his younger brother of a plan which he had formed for making some money by robbing his employer.

' This is my plan, Jim,' said he. ' And a pretty sharp one it is. You see you are a stranger here. No one knows you. Well, you come into the house, and ask for a glass of beer. I'll give you the beer, and when you have drunk it, you put down sixpence on the counter. I'll pretend that it is half a sovereign, and will give you the change that would belong to you for that sum. In the course of the evening, you can come in two or three times, and we'll do the same thing. Then, after shutting up, we can meet and divide the money.'

Jim did not feel satisfied about it, but he would probably have followed his brother's advice, and have gone to ruin, if it had not been for the saving power of ' the truth as it is in Jesus.' As they went along the street, they stopped for a moment by one of the public fountains. It was the one that had the passage of Scripture on it to which I have referred. Jim's eye

rested on it for a moment, and he read the words : ' *The fear of the Lord is a fountain of life.*' He thought of the Sunday-school to which he had been accustomed to go in the country. Many other passages of Scripture at once came into his mind. Turning to his brother, he said :—
' Joe, God will see us. I dare not begin my life in London by thieving.'

The next Sunday he attended a meeting of the Young Men's Christian Association. He took a stand at once against his brother's influence and ways, and soon became a decided Christian. He was saved from sin and ruin. But it was that text of Scripture, 'the truth as it is in Jesus,' that saved him.

LEAVES FROM THE TREE OF LIFE.

The late Rev. Dr. Corrie, Bishop of Madras, in India, was a chaplain there for some time before he was made bishop. At that time, no translation of the Bible had been made into the language of that country, which is the Hindustani. The good chaplain pitied the heathen people about him, who were groping in darkness, and knew nothing of Jesus. To help in scattering a little light among them, he was in the habit of translating striking passages of Scripture into the language of that country, writing them on little scraps of paper, and having his servant distribute them at his door every morning. In doing this, he was, as it were, plucking some of those 'leaves from the tree of life,' which God has appointed for 'the healing of the nations,' and sending them forth on their blessed mission.

Twenty years afterwards, Bishop Corrie heard of at least one instance in which a soul was healed and saved by means of those scattered leaves. A missionary at Allahabad wrote to him, giving this pleasing information : 'I have lately visited a Hindu, who came to this place in ill health. He returned here to visit his friends, and to die among them, after having been many years absent. I was surprised to find that he was not only a Christian, but a Christian with a very clear knowledge of Jesus, and of the way in which He saves the souls of His people. " How is it, my friend," I said to him one day, "that you understand so much about the Scriptures ? You told me you never saw a missionary in your life, and never had any one to speak to you about the way of salvation : then how did you ever learn so much about Jesus ? "

' He answered this question by putting his hand under his pillow, and drawing out a parcel of well-worn, ragged bits of paper, and saying : " From these bits of paper, which Sahib Corrie "—*sahib* is the word which the Hindus used for teacher—" used to distribute by a servant at his door every day, I have learned all I know about the religion of Jesus. These papers I received twenty years ago. I have read them every day, till now, as you see, they are almost worn out. They contain passages of Scripture in the Hindustani language. All I know about Jesus they have taught me ; but what I do know of Him is worth more than all the world to me. It *has saved my soul*." '

And so we see that there are three things that ' the truth in Jesus ' does for us, and on account of which it may be considered the best of all truth. The first is, it sanctifies us, or makes us good. The second is, it satisfies us, or makes us happy. The third is, it saves us. Jesus said, ' I am the truth.' May God help us all to know and love this truth ; and may it sanctify us, and make us good. May it satisfy us, and make us happy, and save us in heaven for ever. Amen !

' I AM THE TRUTH.'

'I SAY, CHARLIE,' SAID WILLIE TO HIS BROTHER, 'ISN'T IT NICE TO BE ALIVE?'—*See page* 124.

VII.

JESUS THE LIFE.

' I am the life.'—JOHN xiv. 6.

IN speaking of Himself, Jesus uses these two little
words, 'I am' so and so, nearly twenty times in
the New Testament. And every time it is done to tell
us something most important about Himself. Each
time that this phrase is used it is like another ray
shining down from the 'Sun of Righteousness.' If we
put all these rays together, how much light they give us
about Jesus! How many wonderful things do they
teach us! We have already had several of these in-
structive sayings of Jesus about Himself. This is the
third that we have had in our present text.

'I am the way,' and 'I am the truth,' we have had
before. And now we have the last of these three
wonderful sayings of Jesus, 'I am the life.' What a
wonderful thing life is! No one can tell how it is that
persons and things are made alive. The wisest men in
the world cannot tell us how it is. But we all know
the wonderful difference there is between live things
and dead things. A dead tree and a live tree,—how
different they are from each other! We see at once the
difference between a dead flower and a live flower, a
dead bird and a live bird, a dead baby and a live baby,

a dead man and a live man. And yet we cannot explain this difference. We say that one of them is dead, and the other is alive. This is true indeed. And it is all that we can say about it. But this does not explain what life is. When Jesus says in our text, 'I am the life,' he means to teach us that He has more to do with life than any one else. No man in the world could say this of himself. No angel in heaven could say it; for it would not be true. But Jesus can say, 'I am the life;' and it is true of Him. And the subject we have now to speak about is this,—*Jesus the life of His people.*

Now there are *four* things that Jesus does for us, which show us how truly He might say, 'I am the life.'

In the FIRST *place, Jesus may well say, 'I am the life,' because He is* THE GIVER OF LIFE.

The Bible tells us that He 'giveth to *all* life.' And we cannot go anywhere without finding living things. Heaven is full of life; for the angels live there. This world is full of life; for, wherever we go, we find people living. And when we go outside of the homes in which we live, we find life everywhere. In the fields, on the hills, up on the tops of the highest mountains, in the ponds and rivers and seas and in the great ocean, far down to its lowest depths, something or other is found living. And the air is full of life. At the close of a summer day, when the sunbeams shine slantingly across some lane in the country, you see, as you walk along, swarms of little insects dancing about there. And it is Jesus who gives life to all these things. The flowers of the garden, the grass and plants of the field, the trees of the forest, the creeping things of the earth, the birds of the air, the fishes of the sea, animals and men and angels, all owe their life to Him. He is called in the Bible 'the Prince of life.' (Acts iii. 15.) And He who

gives life to all creatures may well say of Himself, ' 1
am the life.'

But it is particularly because He gives life to our
souls when they are dead in sins, and makes it possible
for them to live for ever, that Jesus is called ' the life.'

THE FOUNTAIN OF LIVING WATER.

Some time ago, there was a village in England that
was poorly supplied with water. In summer time, the
wells dried up, and the people suffered greatly from the
want of water. About a mile from the village there
was a spring that never failed, but yielded an abundant
supply of excellent water. A good man living in that
village, who was rich, had the water from this spring
brought by pipes into the village, making a fountain
from which the people could always get a full supply
of pure, wholesome water. He did this all at his own
expense. The people of that village were very grateful
to him ; and when he died, they built a monument to
his memory.

But suppose that, in addition to supplying the
people of that village with water when they were
thirsty, this fountain had had the power to heal them
when they were sick, and to make them alive when they
were dead : what a wonderful fountain that would have
been !

And yet such a fountain as this would only be a fair
illustration of what the gospel of Jesus is and what it
does for our souls. It is a fountain whose water has
power not only to quench the thirst of the soul, but to
heal the diseases of the soul, to make dead souls alive
and cause them to live for ever. This sounds very
strange, but it is just as true as that God lives.

BEING ALIVE.

Let me tell you of a conversation that took place between two boys, about the way in which Jesus makes dead souls alive.

'I say, Charlie,' said Willie to his brother, 'isn't it nice to be alive! Why, only see how I can toss my arms about, and use my legs and feet and hands. And, then, I can see and hear and feel. I can talk and sing and laugh, and do so many things.' 'I tell you, Willie, it's real nice to be alive, especially when you are *all* alive, and have no part of you dead.'

'*No part of you dead!*' said Willie. 'Why, Charlie, what do you mean? Whoever heard of such a thing as being part alive and part dead?'

'I have, Willie.'

'That's strange! Who was it, brother? I'm sure it must be dreadful.'

'Indeed, it is dreadful, Willie.'

'Do tell me, brother, who it was that was in this sad state.'

'It was *myself*, Willie,' said Charlie. 'The best part of me was quite dead; and what made it still worse was that I didn't know it. People told me so, but I didn't believe it then. I thought like you that I was all alive.'

'But what part of you was dead, Charlie? I don't understand what you mean.'

'It was my soul, Willie,—that part of me that thinks and plans and remembers. You know that when you shut up your eyes, and stop your ears ever so close, there is something in you that still keeps on thinking and remembering, and being glad or sorry, all the same as though you knew and heard. Do you understand now, Willie?'

'No, I don't; did you stop thinking and remembering, and all that? and weren't you either sorry or glad?'

'I didn't stop thinking or remembering, Willie; and was just like you, sometimes sorry and sometimes glad. My soul was alive enough for other things; and yet it *was dead towards God.* When God spoke to me, I didn't hear his voice, any more than that poor dead bird we saw a little while ago could hear us when we spoke. When God called me to look to Him, I couldn't see Him; and when He told me to love Him, I didn't do it. I *had a dead soul.*'

'Well, how did it ever come alive? Do tell me all about it.'

'Well, Willie, it was Jesus, the dear, loving Saviour, Who did it all for me. When He was on earth, He said, 'I am the life.' And one thing He meant by this was that He had power to make dead souls alive. He sent His blessed Spirit into my heart, to show me that my soul was dead; and that I never could be happy in this world, and never go to heaven when I die, unless my soul was made alive. And then, Willie, Jesus made me see what a wicked thing it is not to be loving Him and serving Him. And then I thought what a dreadful thing it would be never to have my soul made alive, and not to go at last where Jesus is, or to see His blessed face for ever.

'Then I prayed to Him, and said, " O Lord Jesus, do not leave me in my sins. Make my soul alive, and teach me to love Thee and serve Thee, that I may live with Thee for ever." And the blessed Saviour heard me, and ever since He has made me feel so happy! And now I want to love Him, and serve Him, and do all that He tells me to, just as long as I stay in this world; and when I get through living here, I expect to go and live with Him in heaven.'

'Why, Charlie, if what you have told me is true, then *my* soul must be dead too.'

'That's so, Willie.'

'I think, brother, you have told me all this about yourself just that I might go and ask Jesus to make me alive, as He did you.'

'Yes, Willie; that's just what I've told it to you for. Your soul is just as mine was before I asked Jesus to make it alive. We all have dead souls till we come and pray to Jesus. He is the only one who can make dead souls alive. And this is what He meant, when He said, "I am the life." I want you to go at once to Jesus, and ask Him to make your dead soul alive. Then I can apply to you, Willie, the words of that beautiful parable, and say, "*This my brother* was dead, but is alive again; was lost, and is found."

'And when I get home to heaven, I shall have my little brother with me; and we shall live together with Jesus in that beautiful country, where "there shall be no more death, neither sorrow, nor any more crying for ever."'

And so we see that the first reason why Jesus might say of Himself, 'I am the life,' was because He is *the Giver of life.*

The SECOND *reason why He might say this, is because He is the* SUPPORTER OF LIFE.

We have no power to *make* ourselves alive, and therefore we need such a one as Jesus to *give* us life. But when life is given to us, we have no power to keep it, or preserve it; and therefore we need such a one as Jesus to support our life, after it has been given to us. Nothing in the world has power to keep itself alive. And nothing could continue to live, if it were left

entirely to itself. Some things, when they begin to live,
need a great deal more care and support than others do.
Look, for instance, at a babe that is just born, and a
chicken that is just hatched. How very different they
are in the care they require! As soon as the little
chicken comes out of the shell, it runs about, crying,
' Peep, peep, peep.' It sets up for itself at once, and
begins to scratch in the dirt, and to seek and find the
food it requires. But how different it is with the little
infant! It must be fed, and clothed, and taken care of,
or else it will surely perish.

But there is nothing that requires more care and
support than our souls do, after Jesus has made them
alive. We are in a position of great danger. If left to
ourselves, we must perish. In the words of the hymn,
we may each one say for himself,—

> ' My soul, be on thy guard :
> Ten thousand foes arise,
> And hosts of sins are pressing hard
> To draw thee from the skies.'

We need help and support all the time. And this
is one of the things that Jesus meant when He said, ' I
am the life.' He wants us to understand that when He
makes our souls alive, He will give us all that we need
to support the life He has given. If we have a servant
working for us, we can show him the work we want
him to do, but we cannot give him the strength to do
it. Jesus can do both. He not only points out the work
that He wishes us to do, but He gives us all the strength
we need to enable us to do it. He gives us such sweet
promises as these : ' Fear not, I will strengthen thee';
' My strength shall be made perfect in your weakness.'
The Apostle Paul was so sure of the truth of these
promises that he said, ' I can do all things through
Christ strengthening me.' And Jesus has wonderful

power to support His people. He is like a great
mountain in this respect. You know what wonderful
power a mountain has to support everything that rests
upon it. It nourishes the grass, and the plants, and the
great giant trees. Whole forests of trees are supported
on the sides of the mountain, just as easily as you or I
could support a feather or a fly on our hand. Armies
of men, and troops of horses, might march up and down
the mountain, and it would support them all. And
Jesus is like the mountain for His power to support His
people. And He is like the ocean, too. The sea-bird
lights on the waters of the ocean, and they support it.
If you and I launch a little boat, just big enough to
hold us on the ocean, it will support our little boat.
And when men launch their huge iron steamers, by
scores and by hundreds, and load them heavily with all
sorts of freight, the ocean supports them as easily as
though they were light as a piece of cork. And so
Jesus can support all His people. The youngest and the
oldest, the weakest and the strongest, the smallest and
the greatest, He can support with just the same ease.
He supports the mighty angels who stand before His
throne ; and at the same time He can carry the feeblest
lamb in His bosom, and gently lead along the weakest
and the most tempted and sorrowing.

A CHILD'S FAITH.

A little girl, who had learned to know, and love,
and trust in Jesus, was once looking at a picture which,
I have no doubt, most of us have seen. It represents a
rock rising up in the midst of the stormy sea. On the
top of the rock stands a cross. To this cross a female
figure, just escaped from the angry waves, is seen clinging. She seems faint and exhausted, but she clings
closely to the rock. At her feet is seen the hand of

some one still in the water, but grasping a part of the
wreck that is sinking down amidst the waves.

'What does this mean?' asked the little girl.

'It is called "The Rock of Ages," and is intended
to represent Jesus, our blessed Saviour, to Whom we
cling for salvation. You know the hymn says :—

> "Other refuge have I none,
> Hangs my helpless soul on Thee."

'And again,—

> "In my hand no price I bring,
> Simply to Thy Cross I cling." '

'O, yes,' said the child, after a moment's hesitation;
'but that rock isn't *my* Jesus : for, when I cling to Him,
He reaches down and clings to me too.'

This was beautiful! And it is as true as it is beautiful.
We can use many illustrations to help us understand
what Jesus is, and what He does for us. But, however
striking and beautiful these illustrations are, they never
can show us all that is true in Jesus. He is so unlike
every one else; He is so full of love and tenderness and
power to help, that we can only find it all out when we
come to prove Him ourselves. This little girl felt that,
while that rocky cross did very well to illustrate how
strong Jesus is to support His people, and how willing
He is to let poor, perishing sinners take hold of Him, it
did not show how ready He is to stoop down from
heaven, and stretch forth His almighty arm to take hold
of them.

And the second reason why Jesus said, 'I am the
life,' is because He is the supporter of it.

The THIRD *reason why Jesus said, 'I am the life,'* is
because He is THE EXAMPLE OF LIFE.

I

When Jesus came into our world, He had two
things to do for us.   One was to die for our sins :
the other was to teach us how to live.   Both these
things are beautifully taught by the Apostle Peter in
one verse, when he says that ' Christ suffered for us,
leaving us an example, that ye should follow His steps.'
(1 Peter ii. 21).   When Jesus makes our souls alive, or,
what is the same thing, when we become Christians,
then the one thing we have to do, all the time, is to try
to be like Jesus.   We must try to think, and feel, and
speak, and act, as we may suppose that Jesus would do
if He were in our place.   He has gone before us in the
way to heaven.   The marks of His feet are on the road,
and we must try to ' tread in the blessed steps of His
most holy life.'

THE LITTLE GIRL AND HER COPY.

A little girl went to writing-school.   When she saw
the copy set before her, she said, ' I can never write
like that.'   But she took up her pen, and put it timidly
on the paper.   Her hand trembled ; she stopped, studied
the copy, and began again.   ' I can but try,' she said ;
' I 'll do the best I can.'

She wrote half a page.   The letters were crooked.
What more could be expected from a first effort ?   The
next scholar stretched across the desk and said, ' What
scraggy things you make ! '   Tears filled the little girl's
eyes.   She feared to have the teacher look at her book.
' He will be angry, and scold me,' she said to herself.

But when the teacher came, he looked and smiled.
' I see you are trying, my little girl,' he said kindly ;
' and that is all I expect.'

She took courage.   Again and again she studied
the beautiful copy.   Then she took up her pen and
began to write.   She wrote very carefully, with the copy

always before her. Still she was not satisfied. The
letters straggled here, were crowded there, and some of
them seemed to look every way. She trembled when
she heard the step of the teacher. ' I 'm afraid you 'll
find fault with me,' she said ; ' my letters are not fit to
be on the same page with the copy.'

' I do not find fault with you,' said the teacher, ' because you are only a beginner. Keep on trying. In
this way, you will do better every day, and soon get to
be a very good writer.'

' Thank you, Sir,' said the girl, and went on trying
to imitate her copy.

And this is the way we are to try to be like Jesus.
He is our copy. We must try to make our lives like
His. But when we read about Jesus, and learn how
holy, and good, and perfect He was, we must not be dis-
couraged if we do not become like Him at once. We
cannot become like Him in a minute, or a day, or a
year. But if we keep on trying, and ask God to help
us, we shall ' learn of Him to be meek and lowly in
heart; ' and we shall become daily more and more like
Him.

THE EXAMPLE COPIED.

Here is a story of a Christian lady who had learned
well the lesson of being like Jesus, and of the good that
she did by her example. This lady's name was Miss
Bishop. She had been brought up in one of the New
England States. Her parents were rich, and she had a
very comfortable home with them. But she was an
earnest Christian woman. She wished to make herself
like Jesus, and so she gave herself to missionary work,
among the Indians, in the distant North-west. She had
been teaching there for some years. The Indians in her

school loved and respected her.   And well they might, for she had laboured most faithfully for their good. She was kind, and gentle, and very patient.   The oldest of her scholars had never seen her lose her temper. And when she read, and spoke to them about Jesus, they saw that she was following His example, and was living like Jesus.   This made them feel sure that the Bible was true.

But some of the scholars, who had not become Christians, felt uncomfortable about it.   The truth is, their consciences were troubling them for not being Christians.   Miss Bishop's example seemed to be saying to them every day, 'The Bible is true.   You ought to become Christians.'   And they thought if they could only see her get angry once, they would not feel so uneasy about it.

So, after school one day, some of the larger boys had a meeting to talk about it.   They wanted to settle upon a plan to do something that would make Miss Bishop angry.   But they could not agree, and were on the point of giving it up, when one of the boys, Jimmy Corn-planter, whose little black eyes had been looking intently at the clouds, jumped up, and said : 'Me know.   Me no tell.   You come to-morrow morning, and see.   Miss Bishop, she mad !   She very mad !'

None of them believed that Cornplanter could make Miss Bishop angry ; but they all promised to come.

It was in the midst of winter, and that winter was an unusually severe one.   Early the next morning, Jimmy Cornplanter was at the school, and so were the other boys, long before the time for the teacher to appear.   He told them his plan, which was quickly carried out.

This was it : to fill the stove in the school-room full of snow, and then hide themselves, so that, without being seen, they could watch and see how angry their teacher would be when she came to start the fire, as it seemed she was in the habit of doing, and found the stove full of snow.

That morning was bitterly cold. Miss Bishop started in good season to get the fire burning well before school began. She had to make her own path through the snow, and she felt chilled through by the time she reached the school-house. Her fingers fairly ached with cold as she unlocked the door. She thought of the comfortable home she had left, where father, mother, sisters, and brothers were all ready to do everything for her comfort. But she said to herself, 'I am doing it for Jesus;' and that thought warmed her heart and made her feel happy.

She entered the school-room, and taking her little basket of kindlings, she opened the door of the stove to start the fire; and there, to her amazement, was the stove packed full of snow.

She rubbed her eyes, to be sure she was awake. But there it was. In a moment she suspected it was a trick of the boys. Then she calmly walked to the door, and taking the water-pail and the fire-shovel, she patiently set to work to take out the snow, without one angry word or impatient look.

This was too much for the invisible boys, who had watched it all from their hiding-places. They came out looking rather foolish; but after asking the teacher's pardon for their mischief, they took the shovel and the pail, and soon had the snow all removed, and a good, rousing fire in the place of it.

This conduct of their teacher had a wonderful effect on the boys. It made them feel sure that what the Bible says is true. And during recess that day, she heard them shouting in triumph,—'Miss Bishop, she can't mad! Miss Bishop, she can't mad!'

You see how truly Jesus was the example of this good missionary's life. And so the third reason why Jesus might say, 'I am the life,' is that He is the example of life.

There is one other reason why Jesus might call Himself the life, *and this is because He is* THE REWARDER OF LIFE.

I mean by this that, when Jesus makes our souls alive, and teaches us to live for Him, He makes us happier than we can be in any other way. It says in the Bible that '*His reward is with Him.*' This refers to the happiness that Jesus gives to His people in this life. Those who really love and serve Jesus are the happiest people in the world. When David was speaking about the happiness he found in serving God, he said it 'put more gladness in his heart than' worldly men find 'when their corn, and their oil, and wine increase.' Corn and wine and oil were the things in which men invested their money in the time of David when they grew rich. And then, if it was said of a man that his corn and wine and oil were increasing, the meaning of it was that he was getting rich. And the gladness which worldly men feel when they are getting rich is the greatest gladness they have. So that what David meant to say was that the happiness he found in serving God was greater than any he had ever found in this world. And David was a good judge in this matter. He was a great king and a very rich man. He knew all about the happiness that riches bring. And yet he said that serving God made him happier than being rich.

And this is just as true to-day as it was when David lived, three thousand years ago. Let us look at one or two illustrations of this.

SHE GOT HER REWARD.

A minister in England was travelling through the country, holding meetings for the Bible Society. He stopped one day at a village where he had some business, and went to the inn to get his dinner. A nice-looking girl, about fifteen years of age, waited on him at the table. This minister always liked, when he met with strangers, to say something to them that might do them good. So, before leaving, he said to this young girl :—

'What is your name, my friend ? '

' Jane, Sir.'

' Well, Jane, do you ever pray ? '

' O, no, Sir; I 've no time for anything like that. Why, I hardly have time to eat my victuals.'

' Now, Jane, I want to make a bargain with you. I expect to be back here in about two months. I 'll teach you a little prayer, of only three words, which I want you to say every morning. It needn't take any time; for you can say it, if you like, while you are getting dressed. And when I come back, if you tell me that you have said it every day, I 'll give you half-a-crown.'

' I 'll do it,' said Jane; ' I 'll do it.'

' Well, be sure and keep your promise.'

' Yes; you may depend on that, for I always keep my promise,' said Jane. ' And now tell me what the prayer is ? '

' This is it,' said the minister. ' " Lord, save me." '

Then he shook hands with Jane, and said good-bye.

After two months, he came back to that village. On going to the inn for his dinner, Jane was not there, and another girl waited on him in her place. After dinner, he spoke to the person who kept the house, and asked where Jane was.

'O, she took to going to church, and left here, and now she's living at the parson's down the road.'

Then he went to the parsonage. He knocked at the door, and who should open it but Jane herself. As soon as she saw the minister, she lifted up her hands and said,—

'You blessed man! I'm so glad to see you again, and to thank you for teaching me that prayer. But I don't want your half-crown, because I've got enough already.'

'Well, well, let me know what you've got. Come, tell me all about it.'

'You see, Sir, after you went away, I used to say that prayer every morning. At first I said it carelessly, while I was getting dressed, without thinking anything about it. But one morning after I had said it, these two questions came into my mind : What did that gentleman want me to say this prayer for ? what does "*save*" mean ? I thought the Bible would tell me something about this ; so I borrowed one, and read in it a little every morning. Pretty soon, I read one verse, which said, "The Son of man is come to seek and *to save that which is lost;*" and another which said, "Christ Jesus came into the world *to save sinners."* Then I saw that I was a lost sinner. This frightened me. I began to pray in earnest. I asked Jesus to pardon my sins, and make me a Christian, and teach me to love and serve Him. He heard my prayer. He has done all this for me ; and now I'm just as happy as the day is long. And so I thank you for teaching me that prayer, but I won't take your half-crown.'

Now, here we see how Jesus made this girl's soul alive, and then rewarded her by making her life happy.

But it is only a small part of this reward that Jesus

gives to His people in this world. The greater part of it is laid up for them in heaven, and will be given them hereafter.

TRUE RICHES AMIDST POVERTY.

An aged man was sitting by the fire in an almshouse. He was poor and deaf, and his limbs were shaking with palsy.

'What are you doing?' said a friend who called to see him.

'I am waiting.'

'And what are you waiting for?' asked his friend.

'I am waiting for the coming of my Saviour!'

'And why do you wait for His coming?'

'Because I expect great things when He comes.'

'What do you expect He will give you?'

'I *know* He will give me, because He has promised it, "a house not made with hands, eternal in the heavens." "In His presence there is fulness of joy: at His right hand there are pleasures for evermore.' I am waiting for these.'

How well that man might feel happy! He was living in the poor-house indeed; and he was deaf, and shaking with the palsy; and yet he was better off than the richest man in the world, or the mightiest king on his throne, who has no share in the reward that Jesus gives. The story about Jane and her little prayer shows us how Jesus rewards His people in this life; and the story about the poor man in the almshouse, waiting for the coming of Jesus, shows us how He will reward His people in the world to come.

Jesus said of Himself, ' *I am the life.*' We have spoken of four good reasons why He might well say this. The FIRST is because He is THE GIVER OF LIFE;

the SECOND, because He is THE SUPPORTER OF LIFE ; the
THIRD, because He is THE EXAMPLE OF LIFE ; and the
FOURTH because He is THE REWARDER OF LIFE.

Now the best thing in the world for each of us to
do is to get Jesus to be our life. We never can begin
to live in the right way till we have Jesus living in our
hearts and teaching us to live for Him. We have had
three sermons on this one text, 'I am the way, and the
truth, and the life.' Let us all look up to Jesus, and
say, in the words of the hymn :—

> ' Thou art the Way, the Truth, the Life ;
> Grant us that Way to know,
> That Truth to keep, that Life to live,
> Whose joys eternal flow.'

THE BOY DID NOT KNOW THE PRINCE, AND HE REPLIED: 'WHY
SHOULDN'T I BE HAPPY? NO KING IS RICHER THAN I AM.'

See page 152.

VIII.

JESUS THE VINE.

' I am the vine.'—JOHN xv. 5.

THE land of the Bible was a land famous for its vines. They grew in its valleys and on its plains and hills. The people used to make terraces or steps, and then have gardens and vineyards up to the very tops of the hills. This must have made the country look very beautiful. There were vines all around Jerusalem. When Jesus was preaching to His disciples the sermon in which our text is found, He was, it is supposed, on His way from the chamber where He had kept the passover to the garden of Gethsemane, where He was to be betrayed. It was night, and the moon was shining. He probably stopped on the way, under some spreading vine. We can think of the moonbeams falling with their silvery light through its leaves. He looked up and saw the over-hanging branches. He knew how they depended on the vine for all their life and growth and beauty. This made Him think of His people and Himself. And so He used the vine, as He has used so many other things, to teach us something about Himself, when He said, *' I am the vine.'*

When we see a vine with its graceful branches, its broad leaves, and ripening fruit, we cannot help thinking what a beautiful thing it is to look at. And this is

one reason why Jesus compares Himself to the vine
Every beautiful thing that we see in the natural world
around us may remind us of Jesus, and teach us some-
thing about Him.   And it is just so with the vine'
This is another 'ray from the Sun of Righteousness..
Let us study this ray, and see what it teaches us about
Jesus.

Our subject is *Jesus compared to the vine*.   There are
three things in a vine, on account of which Jesus may
well be compared to it.

In the FIRST *place, we find* SHELTER *in the vine;* and
for this reason Jesus may be compared to it.

I suppose there is not one of us who has not proved
the truth of this.   We can all, I doubt not, remember
times when we have been very glad to get the shelter
which the vine yields.   Perhaps we have been taking
a long walk, in the heat of summer, and have found ourselves exposed to the scorching beams of the sun ; then
we have looked round, and have seen a large, spreading
vine.   Its broad, thick leaves make an effectual screen
from the heat of the sun.   How cool and inviting the
shadow of that vine seems !   We sit down there, and
feel thankful for the pleasant *shelter* which the vine
affords.   And this is what Solomon means (Canticles ii. 3)
when he compares Jesus to a vine or tree, and says, 'I
sat down under His shadow with great delight, and His
fruit was sweet unto my taste.'   And if we really learn
to know and love Jesus, we shall often find Him like a
sheltering vine to us.

When we are exposed to danger, when we are sorrowing for our sins, or are in trouble on any other
account, we shall find how sweetly Jesus can shelter us.

Some years since, a lady from New London was on
a visit to a friend in New York.   There was a young

girl in this family who was a scholar in the Sunday-school belonging to the church which her father and mother attended. She was so much attached to her school and teacher, that she was never willing to be absent if she could help it. The lady visitor was going home to New London on Saturday afternoon, by the steam-boat which goes through Long Island Sound; and she wanted very much to have Susan, her young friend, go with her. When it was first mentioned, Susan seemed very willing and glad to go. But when she remembered that it would take her away from her class and her teacher whom she loved so much, she changed her mind, and said: 'No, I had rather not go. I am ot willing to be away from my class.'

The lady urged her to go. Her father and mother freely gave their consent, but still she was unwilling to leave. Her friend took the steamer for New London on Saturday afternoon, and departed. Near midnight, when the passengers were asleep, another steamer, coming from an opposite direction, ran into the New London boat. She was cut down to the water's edge, and sank almost immediately. If Susan had been with her friend, she would have found a watery grave with her. I do not mean to imply that there would have been anything wrong in it if she had gone to New London. I only use this incident to show how God made use of this young girl's love for her Sunday-school, in order to save her life. While in her place in the school, she was sitting under the shadow of the true vine; and she found *shelter* in it. It saved her from the danger to which she would have been exposed, had she gone.

A CHILDLIKE FAITH.

One afternoon, two little children, named Willie and

Fannie, were left alone. Willie was seven, and his sister Fannie was five years old. Their mother had gone into the village, and would not be back till after dark. The children had got on very well while daylight lasted. But when evening came, and darkness gathered round them, so that they could not tell one thing from another, and there was no light but the glimmering one which came from the fire on the hearth, they began to feel a little afraid. Willie, however, who was the big boy, put on a brave outside, and when little Fannie asked, ' Aren't you afraid ? ' said,—

'No; what do you think can hurt us here ? '

But when Fannie began to cry, and came crouching down by his side, saying between her sobs that she heard a noise, then Willie began to feel the need of a higher power than his own to take care of them. Taking hold of his little sister's hand, he said :—

' Please don't cry, Fannie; but let's pray. God can take care of us even if there was a lion right in the room.'

' Why, how could He ? '

' God can do anything, Fannie. Don't you remember what mamma told us about Daniel,—how he was right in among lots of lions, and God came and shut their mouths so that they they couldn't bite at all ? '

' Couldn't they growl, either ? ' asked Fannie.

' I don't know about the growling,' said Willie; ' but I know God could make them stop growling too, if He wanted, for He can do anything.'

' Well, Willie, if He can do anything, I wish He would make mamma come home.'

' Maybe He will, if we ask Him to.'

Clasping her little hands together, Fannie said, ' O God, please to make mamma come home, and make it light, so we can see.'

'Why, Fannie, that isn't the way to pray,' said Willie. 'We must kneel down, and try to think what a big God He is, and how He knows all about whether we have been good or not.'

'Then let's kneel down, and you pray.'

They knelt down, and Willie repeated the Lord's Prayer, and then said: 'Please, God, we know we have been very naughty, lots of times; but we want to be good. Please take care of us, and help us to be good, and make mamma come home quick, for we are all alone: for Jesus' sake. Amen.'

Then little Fannie said her evening prayer,

'Now I lay me down to sleep,' &c.

After this, they rose from their knees. Their fear was all gone, and they felt quite safe and happy till mamma came home.

Now, in doing this, these dear children were putting themselves under the care of Jesus, and they felt He was a shelter to them. It was this which made them feel so safe and happy after they had prayed to Him.

ARMED WITH THE BIBLE.

Some years ago, an elderly man lived in the State of North Carolina, who was remarkable for his piety, and especially for his strong faith in the Bible, and in the merciful Saviour who has given us this blessed book. He believed that those who lived under the shadow of Jesus as the true vine were sheltered and safe wherever they go.

He made up his mind once to take a journey on horseback, through a part of the western country. At this time, that part of the country was very much infested with bands of robbers. The old man knew this

K .

very well; and when his friends urged him to take a pair of revolvers with him, he declined, and said he would take no other weapon with him than his pocket Bible. So he started. After travelling for some time, he reached the State of Missouri. One day he found himself in the neighbourhood of one of the worst bands of robbers in all the country. It was headed by a desperate man, whose name was Jim Stevens. Towards the close of this day he met a gentleman, travelling like himself, alone, and who had thus far escaped the robbers.

The first question this gentleman put to him was,—
' Sir, are you armed ? '

' Yes,' said the aged Christian, drawing his little Bible out of his pocket; ' this is my weapon.'

The gentleman, who was almost loaded down with pistols and bowie-knives, laughed loudly at what he considered the old man's folly. And then, in a sneering sort of way, he said :—

' My friend, if that is all the weapon you have, you had better be saying your prayers pretty quick. The den of Jim Stevens is only about ten miles from here. You will get there before dark ; and he cares no more for Bibles than he does for rattlesnakes.'

They talked together awhile, then each told the other his name, and they separated.

Presently night came on, and it grew dark. The traveller saw a light in a house far down a glen, a short distance from the road. He supposed it was the home of the robbers. But he must have shelter and rest, so he went up and knocked at the door. In a very rough way, they asked him in. It was the robbers' home, and a desperate-looking set of men they were.

But, not at all afraid, he took the seat they offered him, and asked for something to eat. They gave it to him.

Then he sat and talked with them about the country around. By-and-by, the captain of the band, the famous Jim Stevens, came in. Seeing a stranger present, he walked up to him, and said :—

'Old man, aren't you afraid to travel in this part of the country, among the robbers, alone and unarmed ?'

'No, Sir,' was the old man's fearless reply, as he again drew out his Bible, saying: 'This is my weapon of defence. I always read a chapter, and pray too, before going to bed. I know you are robbers; but I'm going to read and pray here to-night, and shall be glad to have you join with me.' The whole band burst out into a loud laugh on hearing this. Not minding this at all, the old man began to read. Gradually they all became silent; and when he knelt to pray, every knee was bowed. It was a strange sight to see that band of robbers and murderers kneeling, and listening attentively to the old man's prayer. When he had finished, they showed him a bed on the floor, where he lay down and slept soundly.

He arose early the next morning, and read and prayed before breakfast. They refused to take any pay for his food and lodging, but thanked him for the interest he had shown in them.

When he arrived at the next settlement, he heard of the death of the gentleman he had met the day before, who had such trust in his own weapons, and made such mockery of the old man's trust in the Bible. This man found a sheltering vine in Jesus. The Bible says, 'It is better to trust in the Lord than to put any confidence in man.' And we may say, as we think of this story, it is better to trust in Jesus than in pistols, or bowie-knives, or any other weapon. Jesus may well be compared to a vine, because He gives *shelter* to those who trust in Him.

K 2

But there is REFRESHMENT *as well as shelter in the vine;* and for this reason Jesus may be compared to it.

The fruit that grows on the vine is the grape. And when grapes are ripe, they are very refreshing to those who eat them. We have spoken of the shelter which the vine affords when we feel overcome by the heat of the sun. But suppose that, while sheltering ourselves from the heat of the sun, and enjoying the cool shade which the vine makes, we are both hungry and thirsty too. We need something to eat and to drink. We cannot feel refreshed without this. We are very glad to get into the shade of the vine, and so shelter ourselves from the sun's heat. But we cannot eat the shade, nor drink it either. True; but there is something else there that we can eat and drink. Look at those fine, large bunches of nice, ripe grapes. We pluck some of them and eat them, and they answer both for food and drink. They satisfy our hunger and quench our thirst at the same time. And then we feel refreshed and strengthened, and we are ready to go our way with comfort.

And so, when we learn to know and love Jesus, we find that He is like the vine, because there is shelter and refreshment in Him. What the Bible tells us about Him is like food to our souls when they are hungry, and drink when they are thirsty. There is refreshment in Jesus for souls that are hungry or weary or in want.

Let us look at some examples of the way in which Jesus gives this refreshment.

A soldier boy of nineteen lay in a crowded hospital after one of the battles of the late war. His arm had to be taken off, and he was sinking under the effects of the operation. He had been hoping to return to the loved ones at home. But now that hope was given up. He must die in the hospital. The chaplain prayed with him, and asked him how he felt. 'Happy, perfectly

happy,' was his answer. ' God is with me when I pray,
and blesses me.' As he was dying, the chaplain was
whispering to him about Jesus. ' He is my Saviour!
He is my Saviour ! O, praise Him ! praise Him ! ' and
so he died. Ah ! Jesus was a sheltering and refreshing
vine to that brave soldier boy !

WANTING TO CONFESS.

Some years ago, the wife of an American missionary
was sitting on the verandah of her house in Burmah,
at the close of the day. A native boy from the jungle
came bounding through the opening in the hedge which
served as a gateway. Coming up to her, he asked, with
great eagerness,—

' Does Jesus Christ live here ? '

He was a boy about twelve years of age. His hair
was matted with dirt, and bristled in every direction
like the quills of a porcupine. His clothing was dirty
and ragged.

' Does Jesus Christ live here ? ' he asked again, as
he crouched down at the lady's feet.

' What do you want with Jesus Christ ? ' she asked.

' I want to see Him. I want to confess to Him.'

' Why, what have you been doing, that you want to
confess ? '

' Does he live here ? ' he continued very eagerly. ' I
want to know that. Doing ? Why, I tell lies ; I steal ;
I do everything bad. I am afraid of going to hell ! and
I want to see Jesus Christ ; for I hear that He can help
poor sinners and save them from hell. Does He live
here ? O, tell me where I can find Him ! '

' But He does not help nor save people who go on
doing wicked things,' said the lady.

' I want to stop doing wickedly,' said he ; ' but I
can't stop. I don't know how to stop. The evil thoughts

are in me, and the bad deeds come out of the evil thoughts. What *can* I do ? '

'You cannot see Jesus Christ, my boy,' said the lady; 'but I am here as His servant to speak for Him.' Then she began and told him about Jesus; how He died to save us, and how He gives His grace and Spirit to help us. No poor man ready to die from thirst ever drank cold water more eagerly than this poor boy listened to what the missionary told him about Jesus.

The next day the boy was taken into the mission school, as a wild Karen boy. And one so eager to learn they had seldom seen. Every day he came to the teacher with some new question about Jesus. And soon he learned how Jesus pardons the sins of His people, and gives them grace to keep them from sinning any more. He was baptized, lived a joyful, consistent life for a short time, and then died a happy, Christian death.

This poor boy needed shelter and refreshment ; and when he came to Jesus, and sat under His shadow as the true vine, he found them both in Him.

HOW TO BE HAPPY.

Everybody in this world is seeking for enjoyment or happiness, but very few take the right way to find it.

There was once a famous king. He had great riches and honours; but he found, as many others had done before, that these things do not make people happy. He heard of an old man, famous for his wisdom and piety, who could tell what we must do in order to be happy. So the king went to see him. He found him living in a very humble way, in a cave on the borders of a great wilderness.

'Holy father,' said the king, 'I have come to you to learn the great secret how I may be happy.'

The old man did not give him an immediate answer. But he rose, and walking out of the cave asked the king to follow him. He led him along a rough path till they came directly in front of a very high rock on the side of a mountain. On the top of that rock an eagle had built its nest. Pointing to that rock, the old man said,—

'Tell me, O king, why has the eagle built its nest on yonder high rock ? '

'No doubt,' said the king, 'the reason is that it wants to be out of the reach of danger.'

'True,' exclaimed the wise man. 'Then follow the example of the eagle. Build your nest, make your home in heaven. Then it will be safe beyond the reach of danger, and you will find peace and happiness all your days.'

Such was the old man's answer. And it was a very wise one. It is just what Jesus tells us, when He says, ' Lay not up for yourselves treasures upon earth, where moth and rust doth corrupt, and where thieves break through and steal; but lay up for yourselves treasures in heaven, where neither moth nor rust doth corrupt, and where thieves do not break through nor steal.'

Here is an illustration of the truth of the wise old man's advice to the king. We may call it

THE HAPPY SHEPHERD BOY.

This boy, though in very humble circumstances, had learned to love and serve God. His nest was built in heaven, and it made him happy. He was watching his sheep one beautiful morning in spring. The sheep were feeding in a lovely valley between woody mountains, and the shepherd boy was singing and dancing for very joy. The prince of the country was hunting in that neighbourhood. He watched the boy for a while, and then called him to him: 'What makes you so happy, my good fellow?'

The boy did not know the prince, and he replied: 'Why shouldn't I be happy? No king is richer than I am.'

'Ah, indeed. I'm glad to hear you are so well off. Now be pleased to tell me what it is that makes you so rich.'

'Well, you see, Sir, the sun up yonder shines as brightly for me as it does for any king; and the mountains and the valleys look as beautiful to me as they could do to a king. I would not give these two hands for all the gold and silver, nor these two eyes for all the brightest jewels owned by any king. Besides, I have everything I really need. I have enough to eat every day, and good, warm clothing to wear, and I make money enough every year from my labour to meet all my wants. And then, better than all, I know that God is my friend, and he is preparing for me a home in heaven, better than any that can be found in this world. Don't you think, Sir, I ought to be happy?'

'Certainly you ought, my boy. No king can be richer than you are.'

It does one good just to think of such happiness as this. Yet this is what Jesus is ready to give to you and me. This is the refreshment we may find, if we come and sit under this shadow. The vine gives refreshment, and for this reason Jesus may be compared to it.

But there is FRUITFULNESS *in the vine;* and this

is the THIRD reason why Jesus may be compared to it.

The vine is famous for its fruitfulness. When we walk under an arbour in summer time and look at the vine which is growing over it, when we see how many bunches of grapes are hanging from the branches, when we remember that the branches which bear those many bunches all grow out of one stem, and that from that stem all the sap flows which supports and nourishes and ripens every grape upon the vine, and makes it so juicy and pleasant, then we can understand what the fruitfulness of the vine is. And Jesus may well be compared to a vine for this reason, because He is so fruitful Himself in doing good, and because He makes His people so too.

In the natural world there are a great many vines. In the spiritual world,—that is, in the Church,—there is only one. Jesus is this vine. And all the members of His Church, in every part of the world, are branches of this one vine. This is what Jesus means, when He says to His people, 'I am the vine: ye are the branches.' And all the power that Christian people have to do good, or to be fruitful, they owe to Jesus. Without Him, we can do nothing that is good. But when we are loving and serving Him and trying to be like Him, then He makes us fruitful, and helps us to do good in many ways. Jesus helps the very least and youngest of His people to do good in some way or other.

A Sunday-school teacher was trying to make his class understand this lesson.

'Jesus is the vine,' said he; 'we are the branches; we get all our life and happiness from Him.'

'Yes,' said a little fellow in the class; 'Jesus is the vine, grown-up people are the branches, and *we young ones are the buds.*'

In the natural vine, the buds do not bear any fruit. But in Jesus, the spiritual vine, even the buds can be fruitful; the youngest can make themselves useful.

BIBLE FIRST.

About forty years ago, a business man sat at his fireside in this city. Near by him, playing on the floor, was his only child, a beautiful little boy. It was early in the morning. The day's work was not begun; and while waiting for his breakfast, the father took up the daily paper to read. The dear child came and climbed up on his father's knee, and, laying his hand gently on the paper, looked lovingly up into his face, and said : 'No, no, papa! Bible first. Bible first, papa.' Very soon after, this dear child was taken sick, and died. As that father stood by the coffin in which his dead darling lay, and when he laid him in the cold grave, he seemed to hear his gentle voice repeating those simple words : 'No, no, papa. Bible first.' He never forgot those words. They were ringing in his ears all the time. He made them the rule of his life. He put the Bible first in his heart, in his home, in his business, in everything. He prospered and grew very rich. He became a teacher and superintendent in the Sunday-school. But in the use of his money, his time, his influence, and in everything, he 'put the Bible first.' He bore much fruit, or did a great deal of good. And this may all be traced to his darling child, that little bud which opened so sweetly on Jesus, the true vine.

The person referred to in this story was the late Matthew M. Baldwin, the well-known locomotive engine-builder.

A GOOD SIGN.

A boy and girl, who played a good deal together, both learned to love the Saviour. One day the boy said to his mother, 'Mother, I know that Emma is a Christian.'

'What makes you think so?'

'Because, Mother, she plays like a Christian.'

'Plays like a Christian,' said the mother, to whom this sounded very odd. 'Why, what do you mean?'

'You see,' said the child, 'she used to be selfish and get angry at any little thing; but now she is not selfish any more, and don't get angry if you take everything she's got.'

You see that dear child had become a little bud or branch in the true Vine, and this was making her fruitful in doing good.

THE FAITHFUL PRAYER.

Two families lived in one house, and each had a little boy about the same age: one was named John, and the other Willie. These boys slept together. Willie's mother was a Christian, and she taught him a prayer and some verses of Scripture, and told him to say them aloud every night before he went to bed. The other boy, John, had never been taught to pray. Now when Willie came to sleep with John, he was very much tempted to jump into bed as John did, without saying his prayers or repeating his verses. But he had learned to obey his mother. He did so on this occasion, and see what good came of it. It pleased God to bless the prayers and verses that Willie repeated every night to his friend John. He was led in this way to think about these things, and to become a Christian.

The two boys grew up to be men. They lived to be old men. They were earnest Christian men, and occupied honourable positions under the government in Washington.

The time came when John was to die. On his dying bed, he sent for his old friend Willie. He told him that it was his little prayer which he used to repeat with a verse of Scripture every night, when they were boys, which led him to become a Christian; and with his dying lips he thanked him for his faithfulness in saying his prayers, as that had been the means of saving his soul. Willie was another little branch of the true Vine, and we see how fruitful he was made.

THE POWER OF KINDNESS.

Some years ago, a neglected, ignorant boy was brought into a Sabbath-school in the city of Chicago. He knew so little that he could not even find the places when called for by the teacher. The other boys found them easily. This would have made the strange boy feel awkward and ashamed, and he probably would not have gone back to the school again. But the teacher was quick-sighted and kind-hearted. He saw in a moment the boy's difficulty. In a quiet way, without calling attention to it, he turned the leaves to the lesson and the references. The boy was spared from feeling mortified. He was touched by the teacher's thoughtful kindness. He felt sure that he had a good friend in him. He kept on going to the school. He became a Christian, and then a teacher. And now that poor, ignorant boy, saved by the thoughtful kindness of his teacher, is Mr. D. L. Moody, the evangelist, who has done so much good in the great cities of England and of this country.

What a splendid bunch of rich, ripe fruit that teacher brought forth on the true Vine, when he showed that little act of kindness to his new scholar!

One more story, to show

WHAT A LITTLE BOY CAN DO.

'I wish, I wish, I wish,' said a little boy, who awoke early one morning and lay in bed thinking, 'I wish I was grown up, so as to do some good. If I was governor, I'd make good laws, or I'd be a missionary, or I'd get rich and give away lots of money to poor people. But I'm only a little boy, and it'll take me ever so many years to grow up.' And then most boys and girls would have put off the thought of doing good till they were grown up. But it was not so with this little fellow. While dressing, he said to himself, 'Well, I know what I *can* do : I can *be* good, even if I can't *do* good.' So, when he was dressed, he kneeled down, and asked God to help him be good and try to serve Him with all his heart that day, and *not forget*. Then he went downstairs to finish his sums.

No sooner was he seated with his clean slate before him, than his mother called him to run into the wood-house and see after his little brother. He did not want to leave his lesson, but he cheerfully said, 'I'll go, mother,' and away he ran. And how do you think he found 'bubby'? He had a sharp axe in his hand, and was saying, 'I chop.' The next moment his little toes might have been off, and the darling child made a cripple for life.

As he was going on an errand for his mother, after breakfast, he saw a poor woman whose foot had slipped on the ice. She fell, and in falling had spilled her bag of beans and basket of apples; and some thoughtless

boys were snatching up her apples and running away
with them. The little fellow stopped, and said, 'Aunty,
let me pick up your beans and apples;' and very soon
his nimble fingers had helped her out of her trouble.
He only thought of being kind; he little knew how
much his kindness comforted that poor woman. She
thought of him after she got home, and prayed God to
bless him.

When he came home from school at night, he went
to the cage and found his canary bird dead. 'O,
Mother!' he cried, 'my dear birdie's dead; and I
tended him and loved him so, and he sang so sweetly!'
and then he burst into tears over his poor pet.

'Who gave birdie's life and took it again?' asked
his mother, stroking his head.

'God,' he answered, through his tears; 'and He
knows best.' And then he tried to wipe his tears
away.

A lady sat in the corner of the room. She had just
lost a lovely babe; and though she knew it had taken
angel wings and flown away to the heavenly home, she
longed to have her birdie back in her own nest. But
when she saw this little boy's patience and submission
to his Father in heaven, she said, 'I'll try to trust Him
too, like this dear child.'

Her heart was touched, and she went home feeling
comforted, and tried to be a better mother to the
children that were left to her.

This dear boy was a branch of the true Vine, and
was bearing sweet fruit. Let us all follow his example.
Let us ask God, every day, to help us to *be* good, and
then we shall find many ways in which we shall be able
to *do* good.

Jesus said, 'I am the vine.' We have seen that

there are three things in a vine on account of which
Jesus may well be compared to it. These are SHELTER,
REFRESHMENT, and FRUITFULNESS. May God make us all
living branches of this heavenly Vine, and help us to
bear much fruit, for Jesus' sake. Amen.

'BESSIE, DARLING, WHAT'S THE MATTER? I THOUGHT MY LITTLE
GIRL KNEW THE VERSES SO WELL.'—*See page* 169.

IX.

JESUS THE PLANT OF RENOWN.

' And I will raise up for them a plant of renown.'—EZEKIEL
xxxiv. 29.

THIS refers to Jesus. It was one of the many
promises or prophecies in which He was spoken of
long before His birth. The prophet Ezekiel, who wrote
these words, lived about six hundred years before the
time of Christ. We have spoken of Jesus as ' the Sun of
Righteousness,' as 'the Light of the world,' as 'the bright
and morning Star,' as ' the Saviour,' as 'the Way, the
Truth, and the Life,' as ' the true Vine.' These were all
rays from the Sun of Righteousness. They all, as we have
seen, shed light on the character and work of Jesus, and
help us in trying to understand what He is in Himself
and what He does for His people.

And now we may take this passage from the
prophecy of Ezekiel, as giving us another ray from the
Sun of Righteousness. ' I will raise up for them a
plant of renown.' Plants and trees are beautiful things.
And every beautiful thing that God has made in this
world is used in the Bible to teach us something about
Jesus our glorious Saviour. Suns and stars, and rocks
and fountains, and fruit and flowers, and gems and
jewels, may all remind us of him. And then we have

L

the trees of the forest brought in to help us in learning about Jesus. 'I will raise up for them a plant of renown.' The prophet Isaiah speaks of Jesus as 'the stem of Jesse, and the branch that should grow out of His roots.' (Chapter xi. 1.) In another place, He is spoken of as 'the man whose name is the Branch.' (Zechariah vi. 12.) He is also called 'the righteous branch' (Jeremiah xxiii. 5); and this 'branch' is said to be 'beautiful and glorious.' (Isaiah iv. 2.) And now we are to consider Jesus as the *Plant of Renown.*

Renown, you know, means honour. How well this word may be applied to Jesus ! How renowned He was for the way in which He was born ! An angel from heaven came to tell beforehand about His birth, and a glorious choir of angels came to sing their anthem of gladness over the infant Saviour, as he lay cradled in the manger of Bethlehem. How renowned he was for His life of usefulness, for His death of shame, suffered for our sins, for His resurrection from the grave, and His ascension into heaven ! And how renowned He is for the place He now occupies at the right hand of God !

But I wish to speak of the renown that belongs to Jesus for what He is doing now, and what He has been doing ever since He went to heaven. Jesus is renowned for the great power He has to do *three* things.

In the FIRST *place, He is renowned for the great power He has* TO HEAL.

One of the special names by which He is called in the Old Testament is 'the Lord who *healeth.*' (Exodus xv. 26.) David said, 'Bless the Lord, O my soul, who *healeth* all thy diseases.' (Psalms ciii. 3.) In another place, when he is speaking of God our Saviour, he says that 'He *healeth* the broken in heart, and bindeth up their wounds;' or, as the Prayer Book version of the Psalms says, 'He giveth medicine to *heal* their sicknesses.' (Psalms cxlvii. 3.) In another place, David says, 'He sent His word, and *healed* them.' (Psalms cvii. 20.) The prophet Jeremiah speaks of Him as the physician who has the balm of Gilead for the purpose of healing the wounds of His people. (Jeremiah viii. 22.) And in another place, Jesus says to His people by this same prophet, ' I will restore *health* unto thee, and I will *heal* thee of thy wounds.' (Jeremiah xxx. 17.)

And when Jesus came into our world, He came as the *Great Healer.* He was renowned for many things that He did, but for nothing more than His power to *heal.* And so we read, you remember, that 'Jesus went about all Galilee, preaching the gospel and *healing* all manner of disease and sickness among the people. And they brought unto Him all sick people that were taken with divers diseases and torments, and those that were possessed with devils, and those that were lunatic, and those that had the palsy; and He *healed* them.' (Matthew iv. 23, 24.)

And when Jesus went back to heaven, He left this wonderful power to heal with His apostles for a while. Thus we read in one place of multitudes of people, with different kinds of sickness, being brought to the Apostle Peter, and he healed them all. And when they could not get close to him, they laid the beds and couches along the streets; and even the shadow of Peter, as it passed over them, had power to heal. (Acts v. 15, 16.) And in another place, we read how ' God wrought special miracles by the hands of Paul,' so that the handkerchiefs and aprons carried from him to the sick people healed them of their diseases. (Acts xix. 11, 12.) No man has the power of healing diseases in this miraculous way now. But all the power which certain medicines have to cure sickness, and all the skill which our best physicians have in using these medicines, we owe to Jesus.

But it is especially of the power of Jesus to heal our spiritual diseases, the sickness of the soul that sin has caused, of which I desire to speak. Jesus is indeed ' a plant of renown ' in this respect. No earthly physician will engage to cure every case of disease that can be brought to him. But Jesus is so renowned for His power to heal, that He is willing to undertake every case brought unto Him, and pledges Himself to cure all.

Three of the most desperate sinners ever known in the world are mentioned in the Bible. One was Manasseh, the wicked king of Israel. We read about his awful wickedness in 2 Kings xxi. Another was the thief crucified together with Christ. The third was Saul of Tarsus, who cursed and swore at the followers of Jesus, and pursued them with cruel persecution even unto death. But Jesus healed all these desperate sinners, and made them loving, and gentle, and useful, and holy, and good. He may well be called ' the plant of renown.' He is indeed renowned for His power to heal all the diseases of the soul.

THE SOUL DOCTOR.

A minister had been visiting a poor sick woman for some time. One day, when he was going up the steps of the house, the sick woman's little girl saw him coming, and he heard her say, as she ran into her mother's room, ' Here comes the doctor.' He was surprised at this, for he thought she must know that he was a minister and not a doctor.

After talking and praying with the sick woman, as

he was going away, he said to the little girl: 'Mary, my child, what did you mean by calling me a doctor? Don't you know that I am a minister, and not a doctor?'

Mary looked surprised and confused; but, after considering it for a moment, she said, 'You're our doctor, anyhow.'

'My dear, what makes you think I am a doctor?' he asked.

'Because,' she said, 'Mother has been sick a long time, and many doctors have been here, and I have had to go after ever so much medicine; but for all that Mother didn't get any better. She used to be so sad; and when I looked at her, I always saw the tears in her eyes. But since you've been coming, she has been growing better. Now she sings, and smiles, and looks so happy. I don't know what medicine you've got, but I know you've been a good doctor to Mother.'

Now this minister had told this sick woman about Jesus, 'the plant of renown.' He had talked to her about His wonderful power to give rest to the weary, and health to the sick, and comfort to the sorrowing. She had prayed to Jesus for these great blessings. He had healed her soul's diseases. It was this which dried up her tears, and caused her to smile, and sing, and be happy.

THE DYING SMUGGLER.

A minister in Scotland had a church near the sea-coast, in a wild part of the country, where the people were very much scattered.

One day, while taking a long walk to see some of his people who lived a great distance from the church,

he saw a storm gathering.   It was likely to burst upon
him before he could reach the next cottage to which he
was going.   Not wishing to get wet, he looked around
for some place of shelter.   Presently he saw, not very
far from him, an old building that looked like a barn or
stable.   Walking very quickly, he reached it before the
storm burst, and went in.   On entering it, he found, to
his surprise, a number of men there.   It proved to be
the retreat of a band of smugglers.   These are men who
live by breaking the laws of their country.   After he
had looked round for a while on that strange set of men,
one of them came up to him and said :—

'Sir, are you not a minister of the gospel ? '

'I am, Sir.'

'Well, Sir, there's one of our poor fellows up in the
loft, who is very ill, and near death, we fear.   Will you
have the goodness to go and offer a prayer with him ? '

'I will, very gladly.'   He climbed up a ladder into
the loft.   There, on a bed of straw, lay the poor, sick
man.   The minister sat down upon an old stool by his
side.   The man was dying with consumption.   He was
wasted and worn almost to a skeleton ; and it was clear
that he had but a very short time to live.

'My friend,' said the minister, 'you and I are
strangers to each other.   We have never met before.
We shall never see each other again till we meet at the
bar of God.   Of course I can have no motive to say anything to you but what I believe to be the truth.   Now,
if I should tell you that I had in my pocket a medicine
that I was sure would cure you of your sickness and
make you well again, would you believe me and take
that medicine ? '

'I would, most gladly,' said the sick man.

'Well, my friend, I have no such medicine to heal
the sickness of your body,' replied the minister.   'But

I have a medicine that will most certainly heal the diseases which sin has brought upon your soul, and make it fit to enter heaven. I will not trouble you with any words of mine. Listen, while I tell you what God has said about this in His own blessed Book. And, while you listen, *believe* the words that you hear, and they will save your soul.' Then the minister began, slowly and clearly, to quote, in the hearing of the dying man, such passages of Scripture as these: ' Believe on the Lord Jesus Christ, and thou shalt be saved.' ' The blood of Jesus Christ cleanseth from all sin.' ' He is able to save, unto the uttermost, all that come unto God through Him.' ' Come unto Me, all ye that labour and are heavy laden, and I will give you rest.' ' Him that cometh unto Me, I will in no wise cast out.' ' For God so loved the world, that He gave His only begotten Son, that whosoever believeth in Him should not perish, but have everlasting life.'

While the minister was repeating these precious words of God, he saw a great change pass over the face of the dying smuggler. The look of sorrow and despair passed away, and a look of calm, quiet peace, of hope and joy, took the place of it. Raising himself on that bed of straw, with his hand lifted up, he exclaimed, ' I believe it,' and immediately fell back and died.

O, surely that blessed Jesus who can heal and save poor, dying sinners in this way, may well be called ' the plant of renown '! He is renowned for His power to HEAL or SAVE.

But, in the SECOND *place, Jesus is renowned for His power to* COMFORT.

If we were travelling through a hot, sandy desert, we should be sure to suffer much from thirst. And the one thing that we should need above all others would be plenty of clear, cool water to drink. And after journeying all day in the heat of the scorching sun, when we came to pitch our tents and stop for the night, if we could always encamp by the side of a fountain of good water, what a comfort that would be to us! Now this world may well be compared to such a desert. We are like travellers passing through it. As we go on in our journey of life, we meet with a great many trials. And just as the heat of the desert makes travellers thirsty, and causes them to long for water, so these trials make us sad and sorrowful; and then we long for something that will be a comfort to our troubled souls, just as cold water would be to our bodies when thirsty. We need a fountain to which we can always turn for comfort under our troubles. But, unless we come to Jesus, we never shall find such a fountain. Jesus is the only fountain of real comfort in the world. If we learn to know and love Him, we shall have a fountain of comfort that will go with us everywhere. How sweet the words which Jesus Himself spoke on this very point! 'The water that I will give him shall be *in him*, a well of water springing up into everlasting life.' (John iv. 14.) We think it a great blessing to have a spring of good water in our orchard, or meadow, or garden, or near the door of our house. And so it is. But now think what a wonderful thing it would be to have a spring or fountain in our own hearts; a fountain, not of water for the body merely, but of comfort for the soul; a fountain that never dries up, and that will go with us wherever we go! He who can open such a fountain in the hearts of His people may well be called '*renowned*.' He is renowned for His power to comfort. Now, let us take some illustrations of the way in which Jesus comforts His people.

THE FATHER'S FACE.

A certain Sunday-school was preparing for an enter-
tainment, in which some of the scholars were to speak
short pieces. In practising for this occasion, a little
girl named Bessie, only five years old, was placed on the
platform to speak her piece. She began very nicely.
But very soon she stopped, looked all round the building, and seemed greatly troubled. Then her lips began
to quiver, and her little frame shook with sobs. Her
father stepped out from behind a pillar where he had
been watching her, and taking her in his arms said:
'Bessie, darling, what's the matter? I thought my
little girl knew the verses so well.'

'So I do, papa; but I couldn't see *you*. Let me
stand where I can *look right into your face*, and then I
won't be afraid.

How beautiful this was! And this is just what
Jesus does for us if we are trying to serve Him. He puts
us 'where we can look right into His face' at all times.
And in that face there is nothing but goodness, and
love, and tenderness towards us. What a comfort this
is!

GOD'S HIDDEN ONES.

The Rev. Dr. Robinson, of the Presbyterian Church,
tells this story. It occurred in his own ministry. I
never met with anything that more strikingly illustrates
the wonderful power of Jesus to comfort His people.

While seeking scholars for his Sunday-school one day,
he found a poor woman, who was living in a closet. It
might be well called so; for it was a little room, opening
into another room,—a room so small that it could only
hold a single bed, with a chair and a little table by the

side of it. The only light in the room came through three panes of glass over the door that opened into the larger room. On the bed in this dark closet lay a woman who was crippled with rheumatism. She could not sit up, nor dress herself, nor help herself to the least thing, nor even change her position in the bed without assistance. The people who lived in the adjoining room, and took the little care of her that was taken, were not her relatives. They did not know to whom she belonged. All they knew about her was that every little while some one called and left a small sum of money to pay for the expense of keeping her in that closet. She had lived there, in just the same way, for *fourteen years.* Once, in all that time, she had been lifted out of that little room for a short time. That was eight years before Dr. Robinson first met with her. There, in that dark closet, with no books to read, with no air fit to breathe, with no power to help herself, with no physician to give her any medicine, with no friend to show her any kindness, and with miserable food, she had lived on through all those years. And yet, when the doctor expressed his surprise, she said, ' *She had had all she really needed.*'

Dr. Robinson found that she was a Christian woman, and had belonged to the Episcopal Church, but she never would tell him where she had formerly lived.

'My friend,' said Dr. Robinson, 'has no minister ever visited you during all this time, to talk to you about Jesus ? '

'No minister ever knew where I was, Sir.'

'Have you given up your faith and hope in Jesus ? '

' O no, Sir ! *for that has been all my comfort.*'

'Have you ever thought that God had forgotten you ? '

'I never doubted Him, Sir; but once, after I had

been very ill, I felt sorry because He did not let me die then.'

'I offered,' says Dr. Robinson, 'to do anything for her in my power; but she declined all my offers. She said her case was incurable, and she had learned not to want anything more than what she had.' He talked to her about Jesus, and prayed with her, for which she was very thankful. He visited her often, and kept a kind of watch over her; but she never would tell him anything further about herself. And when he visited her, she never wanted him to talk about anything else *but the love and grace of Jesus.*

' Remembering how much Episcopalians are attached to their Prayer Book,' says the doctor, 'I committed to memory two or three of the collects from that book, that I might use them in my prayer, as the little room was too dark to see to read. The next time I went there, I introduced these collects into my prayer. She recognised the first sentence with almost a start of surprise. Then she began to join in the prayers with me; and when I finished, she was sobbing aloud, and humble, grateful tears were streaming down her cheeks.'

Shortly after this, she died. Some unknown person came and paid the expense of her funeral, and so she passed away. But could anything show the wonderful power of Jesus to comfort His people more than such a case as this? Through all those long, dark years the thought of Jesus, with His love and grace, was the one thing that cheered and comforted this poor sufferer. She was one of the jewels of Jesus. He was polishing her, and making her fit to shine in His crown of glory at last. And how beautifully she will shine in heaven!

Jesus may well be called 'the plant of renown.'

The second thing for which He is renowned is His power to COMFORT.

But there is a THIRD *thing for which He is renowned, and that is His power to* BLESS.

This is the special work of Jesus. He came into our world on purpose to bless it. When God first told about His coming to Abraham, He said that 'all the nations of the earth should be *blessed* in Him.' As all the water in the world comes from the ocean, and all the light in the world comes from the sun, so all the blessing in the world comes from Jesus.

Let me give you some samples of the kind of people that Jesus, this 'plant of renown,' makes when they feel His power to bless. And you will see in a moment that when our world comes to be filled with people of this sort, it will be a blessed world indeed.

A NOBLE ANSWER.

Some years ago, a negro boy about sixteen or seventeen years of age, who was a slave, but who had learned to know and love Jesus, was put up for sale in one of the West India Islands. A kind master, who pitied his condition, and did not want him to fall into the hands of a cruel owner, went up to him and said :—

'Sambo, if I buy you, will you be honest?'

With a look that I have no power to describe, says the gentleman, the boy replied,—

'Massa, I will be honest, whether you buy me or not.'

That was a noble answer. No prince, no king, no angel from heaven, could have given a better one.

MAKE MOTHER HAPPY.

'Mother's cross,' said Maggie, coming into the kitchen, with a pout on her lips. Her aunt was busy ironing, but she looked up and said: 'Then this is the very time for you to be pleasant and helpful. Mother was awake nearly all night with the baby.'

Maggie made no reply. She put on her hat, and walked off into the garden. But a new idea went with her. She was trying to be a Christian. Thinking of her aunty's words, she said to herself: 'The very time to be helpful and pleasant is when other people are cross. Now's the time for me to try to be useful. I remember, when I was sick last year, I was so nervous that if any one spoke to me I could hardly help being cross. But mother never got angry or out of patience. She was as gentle as could be with me. I ought to pay it back now, and I will.'

Then, lifting up her heart in prayer to God for help, she sprang from the grass where she had thrown herself down, and went into the house. Her mother was minding the baby, who was teething and very fretful. Maggie brought the pretty ivory bells, and began to jingle them for the little one. He stopped fretting and began to smile.

'Couldn't I take him out to ride in his carriage, mother,—it is such a nice morning?' she asked.

'I should be very glad if you would,' said her mother.

The little hat and sack were brought, and baby was soon ready for the ride.

'I will keep him out as long as I can,' said Maggie; 'and you please lie down on the sofa, mother dear, and take a nap while I am gone. You look very tired.'

These kind, thoughtful words of Maggie, and the

kiss that went with them, were almost too much for the
mother.   Tears filled her eyes, and her voice trembled
as she said, 'Thank you, my darling, it will do me a
world of good if you will keep him out an hour; for
my head aches badly this morning, and the air will do
him good too.'

How happy Maggie felt as she was trundling the
little carriage up and down the walk! She was denying
herself, and trying to be like Jesus, 'Who went about
doing good.' And it always makes us happy to do this.
And then she made the baby happy and her mother
happy.   And this is the way in which Jesus, 'the plant
of renown,' shows His power to bless people.   Suppose
we were all trying to deny ourselves, and do good as
little Maggie was, what blessings we should be wherever
we went, and how happy our homes would be!

THE YOUNG MINER'S DEATH.

Some time since, the noise of an explosion was heard
in an English coal-pit.   Those who heard the dreadful
sound knew what it was.   They knew at once that a
fire was raging, and the suffering and death it would
bring to the poor miners.   Crowds of anxious relatives
and friends hurried to the mouth of the pit to seek their
loved ones.   Soon they began to bring up the dead and
wounded from the mine; and sobs, and cries, and
shrieks were heard from those who discovered their
suffering relatives.   There was a poor widow in this
crowd, whose only son was a worker in that mine.   He
was a good, Christian boy, the chief support and comfort of his mother.   Presently she was seen pushing her
way through the crowd, with sobs and tears as she
cried: 'That's my dear lad's voice!   Where art thou,
my child?'   And when she reached him, he said:

'Mother, what will you do now?' for he felt that he was dying. She said: 'I will trust in God: can *you* trust Him, Jimmy?'

'Yes,' said he; 'God is by my side; Jesus is with me.'

She stooped down to kiss him; but as she did so the skin of his poor, burnt face peeled off on her lips.

'The Lord be with you, my boy,' she said.

'Thank God,' he replied, 'that this is not the unquenchable fire! Jesus is with me, and heaven is my home. You'll meet me there, won't you, mother?'

'Yes, my lad; I set out for heaven years ago, and I hope to meet you there.'

Then the poor lad was carried towards his mother's house, but before reaching it he died. The last faint words heard from his lips were, 'Heaven is my home.'

Now there is nothing in all the world that could have had power to bless that poor dying boy and his bereaved and sorrowing mother as Jesus, 'the plant of renown,' did. They knew Him and they trusted Him; and in the most trying circumstances they felt His power to bless them.

BONNIE CHRISTIE.

Two boys were in a schoolroom alone by themselves. One of them, named Bonnie Christie, was trying to follow Jesus; the other, whose name was Sandy Dawson, had no thought nor care about religion. They had some fireworks with them; and, contrary to the teacher's command, Sandy Dawson set some of them off.

As soon as school opened, the teacher called them both up, to ask about the fireworks.

'Sandy, did you set off those fireworks?'

'No, Sir,' was the answer.

'Bonnie, was it you who did it?' But he refused to say either yes or no. So the teacher gave him a severe flogging for being, as he thought, both disobedient and obstinate.

At recess, when the two boys were together, Sandy Dawson said to his friend,—

'Bonnie, why didn't you deny it?'

'Because, Sandy, as there were only two of us in the school at the time, it would have been plain that one of us was lying about it.'

'Then why didn't you say I did it?'

'Because you had already said you didn't, and I *didn't want to fasten the lie on you.*'

Sandy melted right down under this. As soon as recess was over, and school began again, he marched straight up to the teacher's desk, and said, 'Please, Sir, I can't bear to think that I told a lie, and that Bonnie Christie was punished for it. It was I that set off the fireworks.' And then he burst into tears.

As the teacher looked on Sandy making this frank, honest confession, and thought how wrong he had been in punishing Bonnie, his conscience smote him, and *his* eyes filled with tears. He took hold of Sandy Dawson's hand, and before all the school they walked together down to where Bonnie Christie sat, and there, with a great deal of feeling, he said,—

'Bonnie, Bonnie, my lad, Sandy and I beg your pardon. We were both to blame.'

The school was hushed and still, for who can help being quiet when anything good and true and noble is being done? It was so still that you might have heard Bonnie's big boy tears drop, one by one, on his copy-book, as he sat there, enjoying the threefold victory he had gained,—the victory over himself, the victory over his schoolmate, and over his teacher too. He was at a loss what to say, and so he gently said, 'Teacher for ever!' And the boys took it up, and gave a good loud, 'Hurrah for our teacher!' And then they made the school-house ring again with their hearty and united 'Hurrah for Bonnie Christie!'

O, what a blessing it will be to the world when boys and girls, and men and women, learn to act towards each other as Bonnie Christie acted towards Sandy Dawson!

I have one more story. It is about a speech made in a meeting by an old coloured woman, whose name was Sarah. She was trying to show that the best way of overcoming evil was by doing good. But she compared the evil things we are tempted to do to devils, and the good things by which we must overcome them to angels. And this was

OLD SARAH'S SPEECH.

'My frens, this yer way of fighting devils with devils ain't jess the thing. Some one gets angry, and then you get angry too : that ain't no way. Now I tried fighting one devil against another in that way, ever so long ; but it did no good. Devils don't want to kill devils : they only help each other on. If I gets envious because somebody's proud, who gets hurt, I'd like to know? Not the devil, you may reckon, sure. But *now* I fights angels 'gainst devils; and the angels is always sure to beat. When anybody says something bad about me, I jess says : " Now, angels, good angels, I don't know how many of you I shall want to help me, but you must stand by me till this thing is through with, 'cause I must conquer." And when I gets insulted, and the blood flies up above my eyes, I says, ' Angels, be quick, and overcome the devils that 's rushing in.' And they

M

always do help.   God had twelve legions for Jesus, and
He has as much as a dozen for you and me any time.
The angels is the strongest.   The right makes 'em
strong.   There be more for us than there be against us·
I tell ye, all we want is our eyes opened to see some of
these yer angel folks, filling all the hills, jess as they
did .in Elisha's time.   There ain't anything they are
afraid of, because they know God is in them, and for
them.   And we 'll get that strong some day.

'I 'spect dis yer world is mighty full of angels ; and
I jess do hope you 'll call on them to fight your battles
for you.   What they got to do but to help us ?   They
doesn't want to waste their time any more than we do,
jess singin'.   They 's trained to do God's work for Him ;
and that 's what they 's round yer for.'

And it will be the most blessed victory this world
has ever known, when all the people in it learn to overcome evil with good in this way.   And this is what
Jesus, 'the plant of renown,' was raised up to help us
to do.   He *is* a plant of renown, indeed !   He is renowned,
as we have seen, for His power to do three things :
these are TO HEAL, TO COMFORT, and TO BLESS.

How thankful we should be that this renowned
Plant has been raised up for us !   Let us all pray to
Him that He may heal and comfort and bless us.

And, then, let us try to send the knowledge of this
Plant of Renown to others, that they also may be healed
and comforted and blessed !

'I WILL RAISE UP FOR THEM A PLANT OF RENOWN.'

THE PROPER MOMENT CAME. HE TOOK HIS AIM, AND FIRED.

See page 199.

X.

JESUS THE SHIELD.

'I am thy shield.'—GENESIS xv. 1.

THESE were God's words to Abraham. And the God Who spake to the patriarchs and prophets in the Old Testament is our Saviour Jesus Who speaks to us in the New Testament. And so this Old Testament saying about a shield refers to Jesus. He is the shield here spoken of. This is still another ray from the ' Sun of Righteousness.'

'I am thy shield.' A shield was used in time of danger. And Abraham was in danger when these words were spoken to him. He had a nephew named Lot. They had lived together for a long time. At last their families became so large that they thought it better to separate. They did so. Lot and his family went to live in one of the cities of Sodom and Gomorrah. This, of course, was before the destruction of those cities by fire. Then that country was very different from what it is now. It was a rich, fertile, well-watered country. The Bible says it was 'like the garden of the Lord.' (Genesis xiii. 10.) So Lot went to live there.

At that time there was a very powerful king in Canaan, whose name was Chedorlaomer. He was the Napoleon Buonaparte of his day. He had conquered all the kings of that country, and made them pay tribute

or taxes to him. Among those he had subdued were
the kings of Sodom and Gomorrah. They had paid
this tribute for a number of years. At last they were
tired of it, and sent him word that they were not willing
to pay any more tribute. This made Chedorlaomer
very angry. So he raised a large army and marched
down to Sodom and Gomorrah, to punish the rebellious
kings and people. A great battle was fought. Chedorlaomer gained the victory. He conquered the kings of
that country, got possession of their cities, took numbers
of the people captive, and with a large amount of spoil
started on his march for home.

Among the prisoners taken on this occasion were
Lot, Abraham's nephew, and his family. As soon as
Abraham heard of it, he resolved to try to rescue him.
Abraham had a large household. He was a sort of
sheik or chief. So he gathered together all his servants,
and the men who were accustomed to work for him.
They made a company of over three hundred men.
Abraham armed them, put himself at their head as
captain, and marched quickly after the victorious army.
He overtook them before they reached home, and came
upon them suddenly. Never dreaming of any pursuit
or attack, they were feeling perfectly secure. It was
night when Abraham came up to them. Some were
sleeping, some eating and drinking, and some dancing
and feasting. Abraham divided his company into three
bands. Approaching from different points, at a given
signal they rushed down upon that careless multitude
like an avalanche. Terror and confusion seize upon
them. They scatter like frightened sheep and flee.
Multitudes are killed. The captives and the spoil are
all recovered; and without the loss of a man, that
little band of heroes march back in triumph to their
homes.

And just here arose the danger to which Abraham was now exposed. That scattered army would soon rally from their flight. They would inquire what mighty host had come upon them so suddenly. And when they came to find how they had been frightened out of their wits, and out of their prisoners and property too, by a mere handful of men under the command of Abraham the Hebrew, they would be vexed and angry with themselves, and still more angry with him. They would be very likely to say, 'Now come on; let us gather our forces together, and go down and thrash that impudent fellow's life out of him. We'll teach him a lesson that he won't be likely to forget very soon.' This would have been the most natural thing in the world under those circumstances. Abraham saw the danger, and feared it. God saw that he was afraid, and so He came to him and said,—

'Fear not, Abraham; I am thy shield.' He meant by saying this to teach him that He would protect him from this danger. He was able to do this, and He did it. He has the hearts of all men in His hands, and He can make them do just what He wishes to have done. If Chedorlaomer had formed the plan of going after Abraham and punishing him, God kept him from carrying out that plan. And so He was Abraham's shield.

'*I am thy shield.*' These are the words that Jesus speaks to all His people. No one can do so much for our protection as He can. And so the subject we have now to consider is *Jesus the shield of His people.* He is the best shield.

We may speak of three reasons why this is the best shield: *in the* FIRST *place, because* IT IS SO LARGE.

The shields which the warriors had in old times were not large enough to cover the whole body. If a

soldier held up his shield so as to cover his head, he
would leave the lower part of his body uncovered. If
he tried to protect that part of his body, then he must
leave his head uncovered. And even if the shield had
been large enough to cover his body from head to foot,
still it would only protect him on one side at a time.
While he was holding the shield in front of him, he
might be wounded from behind. While any part of
the body is left unprotected, we never can tell how soon
danger and death may come through that very part.

We read about a celebrated Grecian warrior in old
times, whose name was Achilles. It was said of him
that his body was protected all over from head to foot,
so that there was no place in which it was possible for
him to be wounded except in one of his heels. Now we
should think that, under such circumstances, a man
would be pretty safe. And yet the story says that, while
engaged in fighting one day, Achilles was wounded by a
poisoned arrow in that very place, and died of the wound
in his heel.

But when Jesus becomes our shield, He is the best
shield, because He can cover us all over. He can
protect, at the same time, both head and heart, and
hands and feet, and body and soul, and home and family,
and *all* that belongs to us. We see this clearly illus-
trated in the first chapter of the book of Job. There
God is talking with Satan about Job. God praises him
for being such a good man. And Satan said : ' No
wonder he is good, because he is so well taken care of.
Hast Thou not made a hedge about him, and about his
house, and about all that he hath on every side ? '

This was true of Job, and it is equally true of all
who love and serve God. And if we put the word
' shield ' in place of the word ' hedge,' we shall see how
beautifully the words of Satan illustrate this first

point of our subject. 'Hast thou not put a *shield* about him, and about his house, and about all that he has *on every side ?*'

And when we see how wonderfully Jesus can make use of anything that He pleases, in order to protect the lives and property and happiness of His people, we see how well He may say to any one, as He did to Abraham, 'I am thy shield.'

Let us look at some illustrations of the ways in which He sometimes protects His people.

A FRIENDLY WARNING.

A party of workmen were engaged in the Hoosac Tunnel in Massachusetts. One day, as they were resting during the hour appointed for their noon-day meal, they saw a number of rats run by where they were sitting. They all rose at once, and ran after the rats. While they were doing this, a great mass of rocks fell to the ground, just where they had been sitting. They would have been crushed to death if God had not been a shield to them, and had not employed the rats for their protection. He who can save men in this way may well be called a shield.

SAVED BY PRAYER.

In the winter of 1873 there was a terrible explosion of a steam-boiler in the city of Pittsburg. A number of persons were killed, and many more wounded. But there was one life preserved in a very singular way, as if on purpose to show how God can make use of any-thing He pleases in order to shield His people from harm. This singular circumstance occurred to the wife of one of the men who was working in the mill where the explosion took place. She was in her own house, busy with her usual household duties, when she heard the noise of the explosion. All at once she felt an unusual desire to pray. In a moment, she fell on her knees and began to pray. While she was thus engaged, a large piece of the boiler which had just exploded, weighing about two hundred pounds, came crashing through the room, and passed directly by the place where her head would have been if she had not been kneeling down in prayer. That prayer saved her life. Surely He may well be called the best shield who can protect the lives of His people in such strange ways as this !

THE LORD'S WALL.

One winter night, many years ago, the inhabitants of the town of Sleswick, in Denmark, were thrown into great alarm. A hostile army was marching down upon them, and the people were greatly afraid of the soldiers.

In a large cottage on the outskirts of the town lived an aged grandmother with her widowed daughter and grandson. This grandmother was a good Christian woman. Before going to bed that night, she prayed earnestly that God would, in the language of an old hymn, ' build a wall of defence about them.'

Her grandson asked her why she offered a prayer like that, for she certainly could not expect God to do any such thing. She told him she did not mean a real, literal, stone wall, but that He would be their shield and protect them.

At midnight, the soldiers were heard coming, tramp, tramp, tramping into the town. They filled most of the houses in the town. But no one came to the widow's cottage. When the morning dawned, the reason of this was plainly seen. The snow had drifted, and made a wall in front of the widow's cottage, so that it was almost hidden, and no one could get near it.

'There, my son,' said the grandmother, 'don't you see how God has made a wall about us, and shielded us from danger ? '

THE SQUIRREL AND THE ROBBER.

A Christian gentleman once kept a tame squirrel, which was a great pet with him. Bunnie had the freedom of the house, and was allowed to go about everywhere and do as he pleased. In the winter time, he was very fond of making his bed at night in the side-pocket of his master's coat that was hung up behind the door in the sitting-room. He would get a little bunch of tow from his own cage, climb up the door on which the nail stood, run down the coat, spread out his tow-bed, and have the cosiest kind of a nest for a cold night.

Now you would scarcely think that the great God, Who rules among the angels in heaven, would make use of a little squirrel to shield His servant from harm. But He did.

It happened in this way. One night, a robber stole into that house, when the family were all asleep. He made his way into the sitting-room. There he saw the gentleman's private desk, in which he supposed was the money that he wished to steal. If he could only find the keys of the desk, it would save him a great deal of trouble. Looking round the room, he saw the coat hanging behind the door. Perhaps the keys are there. He thrust his hand into the pocket to feel for them. This wakened Bunnie. Not liking to be disturbed, he seized the robber's finger, and made his sharp teeth meet in the flesh of it. The pain of the bite caused the robber to utter a loud cry. This wakened the owner of the house. He rushed downstairs with the poker in his hand, and made a prisoner of the robber before he had time to escape.

And the God Who can protect the lives and property
of His people in such a way as this may well be called
a shield. He can make use of the most unlikely thing,
—an angel, a man, a snowstorm, a dog, a rat, a squirrel,
or anything He pleases, in order to protect His people.
This is the best shield, because it is SO LARGE.

'I am thy shield.' *This is the best shield, in the*
SECOND *place, because* IT IS SO SAFE.

The right word to use here would be the word *impenetrable*. But this is too big a word to use here.
And yet it expresses the very thing in a shield that
makes it valuable. Impenetrable means something that
you cannot get through. In old times, when a soldier
was engaged in fighting, if his enemy raised his sword
to strike, he would lift up his shield to turn aside the
blow. And so, when an arrow was shot at him, or a
spear thrust at him, he would try to ward them off
with his shield. But if his shield were made of paper,
or pasteboard, or light wood, or tin, or even if it were
covered with a thin sheet of brass or iron, it would not
be safe. A heavy blow from a sword, or spear, or
arrow, would go through it. And so, since the inven-
tion of gunpowder, shields are not used any more, because they cannot be made light enough for a soldier to
carry, and yet solid enough to prevent a rifle-ball from
going through. Indeed, it is impossible to make a
shield now of any kind that cannot be penetrated.
Why, even when we cover the sides of our ships-of-war
with plates of solid iron, four and five inches thick,
they are not safe, they are not impenetrable. A cannon-
ball can be sent with such force as to go crashing
through them. But, when Jesus becomes our shield,
we are entirely safe. He is a shield that nothing
can penetrate, or get through.

This is what God means, when He says to His people, by the prophet Isaiah, 'No weapon that is formed against you shall prosper.' (Isaiah liv. 17.) And this is what David means, when, speaking of the care that God takes of His people, he says : 'He shall cover thee with His feathers, and under His wings shalt thou trust; His truth shall be thy shield and buckler.' (Psalm xci. 4.)

Now let us look at some illustrations of the way in which God's people find safety under this shield. There is the case of the good Hezekiah, of whom we read in the Bible. The king of Assyria came with a great army, and besieged him in Jerusalem. He threatened to take Hezekiah prisoner, and destroy Jerusalem. Hezekiah could not help himself, so he prayed to God for help. God sent him word by the prophet Isaiah that He would be his shield, and would defend him and his city. In the night, God sent an angel against the Assyrians. He smote one blow with His invisible sword. In the morning, there were one hundred and eighty-five thousand dead men in the Assyrian camp. Hezekiah had the best shield stretched out for his protection. He was safe under that shield.

THE PERSECUTOR'S DEATH.

A Wesleyan minister, whose name was Stewart, was appointed to preach in a wild, mountainous part of Ireland, in which were many Roman Catholics. Some of these men were very bitter in their feelings towards the Protestants. One night, this good minister was preaching in the house of a farmer, when a very violent Romanist who was present interrupted him several times. After the meeting broke up, with a dreadful oath he swore he would kill the minister before he crossed the

mountain the next day, as he understood he was going
over in the morning to preach in another place.

In the morning, the minister rose early to get a
good start on his journey. The farmer's wife begged
him not to go, on account of the man who had threatened to kill him. He said :—

'No; I must go. The Lord is my shield, and He
can take care of me.' After lifting up his heart in
prayer, he started.

He had passed over the top of the mountain, and
was descending on the other side, when he saw two
men standing in the road. As he came near them, they
seemed to be much excited.

'What's the matter, my friends ?' he asked. They
pointed to a man who was lying by the side of the road,
and said :—

'About fifteen minutes before you appeared in sight
that man came to this place. We were digging turf in
the field. We saw him stagger and fall. We ran to
his assistance; but when we came up to him he was
dead.'

The minister looked at him, and said :—

'Last night that man swore a dreadful oath that he
would kill me before I crossed this mountain. Poor
fellow! he had come here, I suppose, to carry out his
oath.'

'Well,' said the men, 'he will kill no one now.'

This good minister trusted to the best shield, and
we see how safe it kept him.

GENERAL WASHINGTON.

We have a very good illustration of the safety found
in this best shield in an incident that occurred in the
life of the great and good Washington. When he was

a young man, and only a colonel in the army, he went
with the brave General Braddock, who was command-
ing a small English army that was to march through
Pennsylvania for the relief of Fort Du Quesne, situated
where the flourishing city of Pittsburg now stands.

That army had nearly reached the end of its march,
when they fell into an ambush that had been laid for
them by the Indians. There was a narrow pass near
the edge of a forest through which the army had to
march. A large body of Indians had hidden themselves
in the trees around this pass. When the army was in
the middle of this pass, they were startled by a volley
of musketry being fired right into the midst of them.
They halted where they stood. They were brave men,
ready to face any enemy. But how could they fight an
invisible foe ? The firing was kept up. The men were
mown down like grass, without being able to help
themselves. Well, the end of it was, you know, that
army was defeated and driven back. Before this took
place, however, General Braddock was killed, and
nearly all the principal officers fell on that bloody field,
either dead or wounded. Among the few who escaped
was Colonel Washington. But his escape was one of
the strangest things that took place on that memorable
day. One of the Indian chiefs in the ambush tried to
kill him, without success. He said afterward that the
Great Spirit must have been taking care of that young
man; for he aimed his gun at him deliberately a number of times, but always missed him. Washington had
two horses shot under him on that day, and five bullets
went through his clothes ; but none of them hit him.
The reason of it was that God wished to preserve his
life for the great work he had afterwards to do for his
country ; and God protected him. God was his shield
on that day. And this is the best shield, because it is

so safe. It is an impenetrable shield. Nothing can get
through it without God's permission.

Here is one more story to show how safe those are
who have God for their shield.

SAVED BY A DOG.

Many years ago, a gentleman in England, who lived
in the country, kept a fine, large mastiff dog whose
name was Hero. He was chained up during the day,
but let loose at night to guard the place. It happened
once that several sheep belonging to a neighbouring
farm had been killed on different nights. The owner
of them charged Hero with being the cause of their
death. One night, another sheep was killed, and it
was plain that Hero had killed it. Under these circumstances, the gentleman felt that, sorry as he was to
part with his dog, he could not keep him any longer.
So he said to his servant, in the presence of the dog,
' John, get a piece of stout rope, and hang Hero behind
the barn where he can't be seen from the house.'

Strange as it may seem, the dog must have understood what was said; for he rose at once, leaped over
a stone fence, ran off, and disappeared from that neighbourhood.

Seven years afterwards, this gentleman had some
business in the north of England, on the borders of
Scotland. At the close of a winter's day, he put up
for the night at an inn by the wayside. He dis-
mounted and went to the stable to see that his horse
was properly taken care of. Here he was followed by
a large mastiff dog, who tried in various ways to
engage his attention. When he sat down in the hall,
the dog came and sat by his side. He began to think
there was something strange in the dog's manner.

He patted him on the head, and spoke kindly to him. Encouraged by this, the dog put his paw on the gentleman's knee, and looked up earnestly into his face, as much as to say, ' Don't you know me ? ' After looking at the dog for a while, he exclaimed, ' Why, Hero, is this you ? '

Then the poor creature danced and capered about, and licked his old master's hands, and tried in every way to show how glad he was to see him once more. After this the dog remained by his side. On going to bed at night, Hero followed him to his room. When he was about to undress, the dog seized the skirt of his coat, and drew his master towards the door of a closet that opened into that room. The door was fastened; but after a great deal of trouble he contrived to get it open : when, to his surprise and horror, he found the dead body of a murdered man there. He saw in a moment what sort of a place he was in, and what he might expect that night. He made preparations to defend himself as well as he could. He had a pair of double-barrelled pistols with him, and he saw that they were loaded, and primed, and ready for use. Then he fastened his door, and piled up all that was movable in the room against the door. Then he sat down to wait for the murderers, for he was sure they would come. Towards midnight he heard steps in the entry. Then the handle of his door was tried. Finding it fastened, they knocked.

' Who 's there ? ' he asked.

' Open the door,' was the answer.

' What do you want ? '

' We want to come in.'

' You can't come in.'

' We must come in.'

' Then get in the best way you can, and I 'll shoot the first man that enters.'

N

They sent for an axe to break through the door.
While waiting for the axe, the gentleman heard a
carriage drive by. He opened the window and called
for help. The carriage stopped. Four men jumped out
of it. By their help, the gentleman was relieved from
his danger. The men who kept the house were caught
and tried. It was found that they had killed a number
of persons in that way. Some of them were hung and
the rest put in prison.

Of course Hero was taken back to his old home, and
treated as such a faithful creature deserved to be. And
when he died, his master had him buried, and a monument erected over him which told of his faithfulness.

And surely the God who can protect His people in
such strange ways may well say, 'I am thy shield.'
This is the best shield, because it is *so safe*.

'I am thy shield.' *This is the best shield, in the*
THIRD *place, because* IT IS SO READY.

In the days when shields were used, a soldier was
not able to keep his shield all the time in a position to
defend himself. But it is different with the best shield.
Sometimes a soldier would be engaged in other things,
and so not be able to keep his shield about him. But
although Jesus has very many other things to attend to,
although He has the government of the world on His
hands, and the government of all other worlds, yet He
always attends to the protection of His people, and
cares for them as if this were the only thing He had to
do. The soldier would have to lie down and sleep at
night. Of course, when he was asleep, he could not
hold his shield before him. But Jesus, who promises
to be our shield, has an eye that never slumbers and
never sleeps. Sometimes, even when not asleep, the

soldier's arm would be weary with carrying his shield;
and he would be obliged to lay it down while he rested.
But Jesus, our shield, has an arm that is never weary.
By day and by night, at home and abroad, He is our
shield; and He is always ready to protect and keep us.

WILLIAM OF ORANGE, AND HIS DOG.

There is a story told of William, Prince of Orange,
known as William the Silent, which illustrates this part
of our subject very well.

He lived about three hundred years ago. He was
the governor of Holland. That is a little country, but
its people have always been very brave. Philip II.,
who was then king of Spain, was one of the most
powerful kings in the world at that time. He was
trying to conquer Holland, and to make the Dutch who
lived there give up their Protestant religion and become Roman Catholics. He sent an army into this
country to conquer it; but, led on by their noble prince,
the Dutch people struggled like heroes for their liberty
and their religion. When the king of Spain found that
he could not conquer the Prince of Orange in battle, he
tried to get rid of him in another way. He offered a
large sum of money to any one who would kill him.
There are always bad men to be found, who will do
as wicked a thing as this for money. Some Spanish
soldiers, who wanted to get this reward, made up their
minds to try to kill the prince.

One dark night, they managed to pass by the
sentinels, and were going directly towards the tent in
which the prince was sleeping. They were near the
tent. Their daggers were drawn. They were treading
very cautiously, so as not to be heard. But the prince
had a faithful little dog, that always slept at the foot
of his master's bed. He heard the tread of the mur-

N 2

derers, although they were coming so carefully. He jumped up and began to bark. This wakened his master. He sprang up in bed, seized his pistol, and cried, 'Halt! who comes there?'

When the murderers found that the prince was awake, they turned and fled. And thus that little dog saved his master's life. The prince was asleep, and could not protect himself. But He who says, 'I am thy shield,' was there to protect him. He is the best shield, because He is *always ready*.

THE LOCK OF HAIR.

'Do you see this lock of hair?' said an old man one day to a friend with whom he was talking.

'Yes; but what of it? I suppose it belonged to some dear child who is now in heaven.'

'No,' said the old man; 'it is a lock of my own hair, and it is now nearly seventy years since it was cut from my head.'

'But why are you so careful about a lock of your own hair?' asked his friend.

'It has a strange story connected with it; and I keep it because it reminds me of the wonderful care that God takes of His people.

'At the time to which I refer, I was a little boy of four years old, with long, curly, golden locks. One day my father went into the woods to cut up a log, and I went with him. I was standing a little way behind him, or rather on one side, watching with interest the strokes of the heavy axe, as it went up and came down upon the wood, sending off splinters in all directions at every stroke. Some of the splinters fell at my feet, and I stooped to pick them up. In doing this, I stumbled, and fell forward, and in a moment my curly head lay upon the log.

' I had fallen just at the moment when the axe was coming down with all its force. It was too late to stop the blow. Down came the axe. I screamed : my father fell to the ground in terror. He could not stay the stroke; and in the blindness which the sudden horror caused, he thought he had surely killed his boy.

'We soon recovered : I from my fright, and he from his terror. He caught me in his arms, and looked at me from head to foot to find the wound which he thought he must have given me. Not a drop of blood nor a scar was to be seen. He knelt down upon the grass, and gave thanks to God for this wonderful preservation. Then he took up his axe and looked at it, and found a few hairs upon its edge. He turned to the log he had been splitting; and there was a single lock of his boy's hair. It was sharply cut through, and laid upon the log. *This was the lock.* Do you wonder now that I keep it, and set store by it? What a wonderful escape that was ! It was just as if an angel's hand had turned aside that axe. And who shall say it did not? It is just what we might expect of them. My father kept this lock all his days to remind him of God's care. He gave it to me on his dying bed. I keep it as a precious treasure. I love to look at it. It tells me of my father's God, and mine. It encourages me to trust in Him, and shows me how wonderfully He shields and protects His people.'

He is the best shield, because He is a shield always ready.

One more story to show how ready this best shield is for our protection. The scene of this story lay in India. We may call it—

BENNIE AND THE TIGER.

A dear little English boy, named Bennie, lay sleeping in the shady verandah of his Indian home. The nurse who had been trusted with him had neglected her charge, and left him while he was asleep. A great, fierce tiger, prowling in search of prey, finding the village very quiet, had ventured in among the dwellings. The English gentlemen were all absent, the natives were in the rice-fields, and the ladies were taking their rest during the heat of the day.

The tiger crept noiselessly past the quiet house, until he saw the sleeping child. Then with one bound he sprang upon him, grasped the flowing white robe of the child in his teeth, and darted off with it to his native jungle. Having secured his prize, he laid it down; and as the kitten often plays with a captive mouse before devouring it, so the tiger began sporting with the child. He walked round and round him, laid first one paw and then another gently on his plump, little limbs, and looked into the boy's beautiful face, as if his savage heart was almost melted by its sweetness.

There was a brave little heart in Bennie, for he did not seem to be at all alarmed by his strange companion. He was well used to Nero, the large, black housedog; the ponies were his chief favourites; and he felt inclined to look on the tiger as if he were only Nero's brother. And when the tiger glared at him with his great fiery eyeballs, or when the sight of his dreadful teeth made his heart beat for a moment, he only returned the gaze, saying in baby language, ' I 'm not afraid of you, for I 've got a father ! You can't hurt Bennie,— Bennie 's got a mamma ! ' O, if we could only have the same trust in our heavenly Father, how well it would be for us !

All this time, while her darling boy was in such dreadful danger, his mother was sleeping. The faithless nurse returned by-and-by, to find the child gone. In her fright, she flew from house to house in search of him. But the eye that never sleeps was watching that dear child. The best shield was stretched over him. An aged native had heard the tiger give a low, peculiar growl, from which he knew that he had seized some prey. Taking his gun, he followed in his trail till he came near him. Then he hid himself carefully behind the bushes. He saw the terrible creature playing with the child, and dreaded every moment to see him tear it to pieces. He watched his opportunity to fire, fearful lest the ball intended for the tiger should hit the child. The proper moment came. He took his aim, and fired. The tiger leaped, gave a howl of pain, ran a few steps, and fell dead by the side of the now frightened child.

It was He who said, 'I am thy shield,' who watched over and protected that little one in such an hour of fearful danger. This is the best shield, for three reasons. In the first, because it is SO LARGE; in the second, because it is SO SAFE; and in the third place, because it is SO READY.

Let us be sure that we make Jesus our friend. Then, wherever we go and wherever we stay, we shall be safe, because we shall have this best shield for our protection. Remember that Jesus has said :—

'I AM THY SHIELD.'

HAYMAN BROTHERS AND LILLY, HATTON HOUSE, FARRINGDON ROAD, E.C.

SGCB Titles for the Young

Solid Ground Christian Books is honored to be able to offer over a dozen uncovered treasure for children and young people.

The Safe Compass and How it Points by Richard Newton is another gem from the heart of "the Prince of preachers to the young."

Bible Warnings: *Sermons to Children on Dangers that lie along their Path and How to Avoid Them* by Richard Newton is the sequel to *Bible Promises* that you hold in your hand. Fifteen brilliant chapters. Newton at his very best!

Bible Promises: *Sermons to Children on God's Word as our Solid Rock* by Richard Newton directs children to rest in the certain promises of God.

Heroes of the Reformation by Richard Newton is a unique volume that introduces children and young people to the leading figures and incidents of the Reformation. Spurgeon called him, *"The Prince of preachers to the young."*

Heroes of the Early Church by Richard Newton is the sequel to the above-named volume. The very last book Newton wrote introduces all the leading figures of the early church with lessons to be learned from each figure.

The King's Highway: *Ten Commandments to the Young* by Richard Newton is a volume of Newton's sermons to children. Highly recommended!

The Life of Jesus Christ for the Young by Richard Newton is a double volume set that traces the Gospel from Genesis 3:15 to the Ascension of our Lord and the outpouring of His Spirit on the Day of Pentecost. Excellent!

The Child's Book on the Fall by Thomas H. Gallaudet is a simple and practical exposition of the Fall of man into sin, and his only hope of salvation.

The Child's Book on Repentance by Thomas H. Gallaudet is a simple and practical exposition of the Fall of man into sin, and his only hope of salvation.

The Child's Book on the Soul by Thomas H. Gallaudet is a simple and practical exposition of the Fall of man into sin, and his only hope of salvation.

The Child at Home by John S.C. Abbott is the sequel to his popular book *The Mother at Home*. A must read for children and their parents.

My Brother's Keeper: *Letters to a Younger Brother* by J.W. Alexander contains the actual letters Alexander sent to his ten year old brother.

The Scripture Guide by J.W. Alexander is filled with page after page of information on getting the most from our Bibles. Invaluable!

Feed My Lambs: *Lectures to Children* by John Todd is drawn from actual sermons preached in Philadelphia, PA and Pittsfield, MA to the children of the church, one Sunday each month. A pure gold-mine of instruction.

Truth Made Simple: *The Attributes of God for Children* by John Todd was intended to be a miniature Systematic Theology for children. Richard Newton said that Dr. Todd taught him how to teach children. Practical and crystal clear!

The Young Lady's Guide by Harvey Newcomb will speak directly to the heart of the young women who desire to serve Christ with all their being.

The Chief End of Man by John Hall is an exposition and application of the first question of the Westminster Shorter Catechism. Full of rich illustrations.

Call us Toll Free at 1-877-666-9469
Send us an e-mail at sgcb@charter.net

Printed in the United States
48153LVS00009BA/76-87